PASTOR T's DISCONTENT
The MISSIONAL QUEST!

Written by

Richard N. Lennes

As We Go Ministries, Inc.

PASTOR T's DISCONTENT

Published by *As We Go Ministries, Inc.*

Copyright © 2013 *As We Go Ministries, Inc.*

All rights reserved.

Printed in the United States of America.

ISBN: 978-0-9890471-0-4

Spiritual quotations are from several Bible versions as noted. Used by permission. All rights reserved.

Scripture taken from the *HOLY BIBLE, NEW INTERNATIONAL VERSION®*, Copyright ©1973, 1978, 1984 by International Bible Society. Used by permission of Zondervan. All rights reserved.
Scripture taken from the *New King James Version*. Copyright © 1979, 1980, 1982 by Thomas Nelson, Inc. Used by permission. All rights reserved.
Scripture taken from *THE MESSAGE*. Copyright © 1993, 1994, 1995, 1996, 2000, 2001, 2002. Used by permission of NavPress Publishing Group.

This book may not be reproduced in whole or in part by any means whatsoever without written permission from:

As We Go Ministries, Inc.
1175 Oakwood Court
Hutchinson, MN 55350

TABLE OF CONTENTS

Thank you! 4
From the Author 5
Chapter 1—Break Away! 7
Chapter 2—Start with the Destination! 17
Chapter 3—Love God! 29
Chapter 4—Get on Board! 43
Chapter 5—Serve! 57
Chapter 6—Glorify Whom? 71
Chapter 7—Love Each Other! 87
Chapter 8—Called! 101
Chapter 9—Surrender! 117
Chapter 10—Go! 131
Chapter 11—Trust! 149
Chapter 12—Tell Your Story! 163
Chapter 13—Intentional! 179
Chapter 14—Use God's Gifts! 193
Chapter 15—Strategic! 213
Chapter 16—Interactive Process! 231
Chapter 17—Scope of Influence! 245
Notes 259

Thank you!

Many pastors and super-strong Christians have had a tremendous influence on me over the years. A sincere thank you to those who mentored, taught, and encouraged me. I have no bragging rights to be considered in the class of people mentioned above. As a lay person, I have spent seventy-six years working at developing a loving and Christian relationship with God. At times I got so consumed doing church work that I was distracted from doing the work of the church.

I'm indebted to many, especially my wife, Sandy, to whom I dedicate this book. Her love and encouragement in our fifty-four years of marriage has been the foundation for our relationship and our faith in Jesus Christ as our Savior.

Our three children have been a motivating influence and their support has touched my heart. A special thank you to the Reverend Jeffrey Miller, the Reverend Greg Finke, the Reverend Dean Mahlum, the Reverend Dr. Peter Meier, Paul Berg, Les Young, Kay Johnson, Arlene Benshoof, and Shannon Pennefeather Gardner who have advised and encouraged me in the technical aspects of writing *Pastor T's Discontent*.

Soli Deo Gloria

From the Author

My book title, *Pastor T's Discontent—The Missional Quest*, is the result of how I've seen some churches struggle with their missional quest. A lot of good intentions are poured into serving God and His people in a missional effort, but often well-meaning church leaders see *missional* as church recruitment or appointing a committee for evangelism. They then sit back and say, "We got it covered."

In this book, Pastor T makes a commitment be a missional leader—to equip disciples in the church to be sent outside the church to make more disciples: preparing people to create Christian relationships at home, at work, at social events, on vacations, and on the global stage. His heart is opened to people like JJ, a musically talented street kid, who said, "Dude, you're cool, but your church music is like—for wimps." Many want to learn about Jesus but have no interest in the organized church.

As you begin your missional journey with my fictional characters, keep in mind it is not just a story. It is a Christian blend of God's gift of salvation, obedience to His Word, and our responsibility as believers. Pastor T's view of a believer's life journey is

-Energized Spiritual Growth

-Ignited Relationships

-Selfless Serving

All this leads to Pastor T's vision of "Go—Light the World," derived from our Biblical mission, "Go—Make Disciples." The story-line sometimes makes this process look easy. As a lay person involved in many organizations, I don't want to lead anyone to believe it's simple. However, I do believe simplicity and clarity are possible through the process gleaned in each of the seventeen chapters.

My authorship usually is technically oriented designing a "how-to" approach and exact steps to follow. My writing style with **Pastor T's Discontent** is a deviation from the technical to a process-oriented frame of reference. Technical components of this book are available in other *As We Go Ministries, Inc.* publications.

As a lay person, I felt compelled to witness my view of missional as living out my faith wherever I am and whatever I am doing—inside and outside the church 24/7. It means getting out of my comfort zone, discerning a need, and serving.

Again, *Pastor T's Discontent* is not just a story; it is a message with missional insights highlighting real issues. Each chapter has a Biblical theme ending in thought-provoking questions for the reader to grow in Christ. It can also be adapted to a small-group curriculum with transformational qualities over an eight-week period or longer. Most of all, it is what I would like my church to be—every believer being the church in the community, reaching out beyond the walls and barriers creating Christian relationships as we go in life. I pray that you find this message compelling and find ways in your life and in your church to move toward achieving a missional ministry.

In Christ,
Richard N. Lennes
As We Go Ministries, Inc.

Chapter 1—Break Away!

"And you shall know the truth, and the truth shall make you free."
John 8:32 *(NKJV)*

Each of us has only one motivation to break away—that's to free us from something! Reality of life embeds guilt, failure, and faults driving us to search for that "Break Away" to make our life whole. Finding the truth of Jesus frees us and allows us to find a new life to become who we are intended to be.

Chapter 1 introduces us to Pastor T, who feels called to "Break Away!" In search of his missional quest, he finds a young woman leading a "Break Away" cause in the most unexpected venue.

Break Away!

In his plaid shirt, jeans, and tennis shoes, Pastor T strolled down the sidewalk in front of his church to a nearby neighborhood called the "Village." It was a section of the community that attracted a diversity of people interested in the art—ranging from music to poetry—and bustled with artistic expression.

Rarely venturing into the Village, the pastor chose this five-block journey as a retreat to walk off the fudge he just ate and to try to gain a perspective on some struggling ministries in the church where he was lead pastor. In recent years of his ministry he experienced frustration over the opportunity to steer his congregation to live out their faith as a living sacrifice to God. Lately he experienced a passion to step up his leadership to comply with Jesus' command in the Great Commission (Matthew 28:19 *NKJV*) to "Go, make disciples..." He just didn't know how God was going to equip and empower him with this bold endeavor while remaining in compliance with the truth of the Law and Gospel. For months T had been praying for direction from God to guide him to be more missional himself. Pastor was certain of only one thing: he needed to set the missional example.

As he entered the cobblestone street of the Village, his deep thoughts were interrupted by the street music, mimes, and joyous atmosphere. He sat down on a park bench to simply absorb the hustle and bustle of the quaint community. Resting his elbows on the back of the bench and peering over his glasses at the beautiful setting, he observed clowns, jugglers, gymnasts, musicians, and others performing in the streets. Pastor T smiled at God's handiwork. A young woman with long blond hair and a painted smiling face handed him a balloon on a string. The words "Jesus sets you free!" were printed on the balloon.

Thanking the woman, T removed his glasses and said, "Can I ask you a question?" With a welcoming smile she responded, "Sure, my name is Leah."

"Tell me, Leah," T asked. "What is the big event today?"

"No event, sir," she said. "We're just expressing how God made us. It's cool—you might think of us as God's artists."

"That's great. Are you from a church?" he asked out of curiosity.

"Nope! Nothing like that, we just feel close to God when we use what He gave us."

"I'm impressed." Pastor T inquired, "Leah, what do you know about Jesus?"

"Oh, He's my hero," she said with heartfelt conviction. "He saved me. Hey, gotta go! God bless your day."

Leah skipped off to give more balloons to people on the street. Pastor was left staring at the balloon, wondering what just happened. Something in his heart felt good that this beautiful girl was expressing her faith, but was this missional community? Was it made up of followers who really recognize their community as a place to serve, regularly engaging in the needs of people by giving a part of themselves? Or was it just an afternoon of "rah, rah" activities using Jesus as a torch to ignite emotions?

Putting his glasses in his pocket, T left the Village and returned to his office. After work, he took the balloon that Leah had given him and drove home. Walking in the door, he handed the balloon to his wife and said, "Hey, Lil, Jesus sets you free!" Throwing her hands in the air, she said, "Hallelujah, Amen—but what's your point! You're acting a little weird. Can we talk about this over dinner before the food gets cold?"

During the table prayer he held Lil's hand. T thanked God for placing him in the Village at that moment that day and asked for wisdom and discernment as he searched for opportunity in the experience. As they ate the warmed-up chili and grilled cheese sandwiches Lil had fixed, T told her about his encounter in the Village.

Lil, wiping her mouth with a napkin, said, "Sounds like you had a more exciting day than I did. What's your take on this Village thing?"

"You know, Lil, I'm not certain. It made me feel great that these young people were celebrating Jesus, but are they just doing it as a political gesture to promote their life in the Village? I'd like to think that they really see Jesus as their Savior and are reaching out to serve their community."

As Lil filled her coffee cup, she inquired, "Where's God leading you with this?"

"I wish I knew. You asked for my reaction. Well, I believe God put me there for a reason. What I don't know is if it's a growth opportunity for me or if I was placed there to provide spiritual clarity. Either way, God expects me to take some action."

"How are the leaders in the church going to look at this," Lil asked frowning. "In spite of your vision to transform the congregation to outward serving, their paradigm is still inward. I hate to say it, but we are a 'serve ourselves' church."

"Yes, you're right, but God may have something different in mind. I'm ready to face that risk, and I believe there are some leaders I have been working with who will welcome a bold outreach approach. Not following God's lead on this would be an insult to Him and possibly a missed opportunity for me, our leadership, and our congregation."

Standing to clear the table, Lil turned and said, "Well, I have faith! As you take that step of faith beyond the norm of our congregation, the Holy Spirit will release His power to guide you. I hope He changes our church leaders, too."

"Thanks for your encouragement and for the great chili, Lil," T said, carrying some dishes to the sink. "I'm going to wander down to the Village tomorrow to see if anyone will talk with me. After fifteen years of ministering internally, I have become too comfortable. Getting outside of my comfort zone is both frightening and invigorating."

As T normally did after dinner, he filled his favorite coffee mug with coffee and retreated to his study. His brother had given him the captain's mug, telling T the anchor and treasure chest on the side of the cup symbolized the treasures of God's promises that their father had taught them. That night Scripture, meditation, and prayer were especially meaningful to him as he spent about two hours in his study. With a clear direction and a passionate heart, he was ready.

Morning came and T couldn't wait to visit the Village. Driving his four-year-old red pickup to work was a routine, but this morning it seemed special—he was on a mission! At least until his cell phone rang. There had been a car accident, and his mind switched to urgency for one of his church families.

He rushed to the hospital and ran up the hall to the surgical unit, where he met Todd's family. They told him Todd was in surgery with internal bleeding and a head injury. Pastor T hugged both parents while he prayed for healing from God. A surgical nurse came out of the double doors and told them Todd was still in critical condition. The bleeding was under control, but the doctor was going to keep him in a medically induced coma until the swelling in the brain subsided.

Todd's parents told T what they knew about the accident involving their nineteen-year-old son. Todd was on his way to classes at the college that morning when he was "T-boned" at an intersection. The other driver was killed.

The three of them clasped hands and stood in a circle as each prayed aloud. Pastor T listened to Todd's mother as she praised God for His blessings and pleaded with Him for her son's recovery; then she did something rather surprising under the circumstances. She prayed for the family of the man who died in the accident. T thought to himself, "Now that shows a forgiving heart. She was able to remove her anger and replace it with forgiveness." Mark 14:36 came to mind, when Jesus fell to the ground praying to God the Father in Gethsemane, "...all things are possible for You. Take this cup away from Me; nevertheless, not what I will, but what You will" *(NKJV)*.

They heard someone running down the hall toward them. A frantic voice cried out, "How is he? How is he?" A woman ran right into the arms of Todd's parents as they updated her on their son's condition. The tearful woman told them that word of the accident had spread throughout the campus. She had heard it from a friend who saw the EMTs taking Todd in the ambulance.

Pastor T couldn't believe his eyes. It was Leah, the young woman from the Village. Leah was introduced as a good friend of Todd's, and she recognized T as the person on the park bench the previous day. "Cool! You're the guy I gave the balloon to in the Village, right?"

"Yes, Leah, that's correct. You made quite an impression on me. Have you known Todd long?"

"About two years. We met at a Bible camp. I have been feeling bad about rushing off yesterday without talking more about Jesus. Are you a pastor?"

"Correct, Leah," Pastor T humbly asserted. "After the enthusiasm you showed for Jesus yesterday, I wanted to talk with you again. Maybe we can talk later?"

"Hey, I'd like that. However, let me tell you that Todd has tried to get me to church for two years, and it's not my shelter." Leah turned to Todd's parents and hugged them again as they shared some tears.

The doctor walked toward them wearing his surgical garb. He told the parents and Leah that Todd had a guardian angel. His injuries were serious, but he should recover. Only time would tell about the head injury. While expressing his concern, the doctor also said that Todd would be brought out of the coma in a few days, depending on the degree of swelling. He had taken a tremendous blow to the head, but fortunately the images of the brain showed no permanent damage. A number of staff would be watching him very closely.

With her hands folded at her chest, Leah looked up and said, "Thank God!—and thank you, doctor. When can we see Todd?" The doctor answered, "It'll take about two hours in recovery before Todd will be taken to ICU. The surgical waiting room attendant will keep you informed and direct you to that area of the hospital."

Seizing the moment, T extended the invitation, "Let's give glory to God for watching over Todd." Hand in hand they prayed.

Pastor T gave Todd's parents his calling card and told them to call him personally if they needed him. T also gave Leah his card, saying, "You can teach me a lot about your ministry in the Village. Let's keep in touch. You can call or text me. I'd also like to meet some of your friends."

Driving back to the church, T looked up to the heavens and said, "God, are You messing with my plan?" What was expected to be a simple visit to the Village resulted in a complex and stressful morning. Why such a tragic accident? Why did it have to take a life? Why do bad things happen to good people? Why did it involve Leah?

Almost to the church, Pastor T looked up again and said, "I should have known You had a plan. Although I don't understand it, I know Your plan will turn out better than mine."

He arrived just in time for the weekly staff meeting. As he updated staff on the accident, T suddenly realized he had an opportunity to cast a vision to his staff on the significance of reaching out beyond the walls of the church. He cited Leah and her perception of the formal church. T stressed opportunity to journey with God on the Biblical mission of making disciples. Reactions from his staff were not too surprising:

Worship coordinator Jon said "I hear you, Pastor, but my plate is full! I'm working sixty hours a week just trying to keep up with our own members."

"We had better make time," Phil, the youth coordinator, insisted. "We should all set the example to create Christian relationships in our community and beyond."

Administrative assistant Sue hopped in the conversation with, "I respect what you are trying to do, Pastor, but it seems that they should join our church first. Until then, they are not like us."

"I only clean around here, but isn't this why we are a congregation?" said Virg, lead custodian. "Some people act like church is a status thing. As followers of Jesus, didn't we sign up for the opportunity to serve outside the church in our neighborhood, community, and beyond?"

The comments were bittersweet to Pastor T. He had to bite his tongue at some of the remarks, but he knew this would be a process and that all of his staff had a serving heart and would do the right thing. He also realized there was some burn out from the constant pressures of internal ministry. Choosing a posture of patience, T spoke of God's will and where He might be leading staff and the congregation. He asked each person to consider what his or her role might be in a community-based discipleship effort. Sue was directed to place "Missional Community" on the next staff agenda, and T requested Phil to facilitate staff in an in-depth discussion of the topic next week.

Following the staff meeting, Pastor T had a budget meeting scheduled with the congregational president, Mike, at a local cafe. T wanted to create a budget line item for "Community Missional Projects" and invite Mike to participate in the staff discussion next week. Mike, an accountant, viewed most everything as "income" and "expense," and it was going to be a challenge discussing "Missional Investment."

As he trucked over to the café, T decided that he would wait until the impact of the accident settled before he visited the Village. He was sad the way things worked out, but he also knew that God had a bigger and better plan. He rejoiced over the faith he had observed in Todd's parents and the fact that Leah apparently had a Christian background. Still experiencing a feeling of adventure beyond the walls of the church, Pastor T knew God was in control and patience was the virtue for the moment. He smiled and focused on John 8—as he thought about Leah's balloon message of a believer knowing the divine truth and freedom from sin.

LOOKING FOR MEANING:

1. Why is it that in our lives we sometimes experience things happening when we least expect it? What are some examples of that in this chapter? How about in your life?

2. Identify the different circumstances in this chapter where there is evidence of someone stretching his or her faith. How do you stretch your faith in your life journey?

3. Why is it difficult to get people in the church to serve outside of the church? What would you say the purpose of the church is?

Chapter 2—Start with the Destination!

"Go therefore and make disciples of all the nations…"
Matthew 28:19 *(NKJV)*

On the basis of Jesus' authority, His disciples were sent to make disciples. We are sent also, by the same command, to make disciples wherever we go. Going beyond the walls of the church requires stepping out of our comfort zone to influence people's lives in the true Biblical mission of the church.

In Chapter 2 we find a supportive pastor's wife encouraging her husband to fulfill his passion to think, talk, and act missionally. Pastor T knows that he will have no influence with his congregation unless he submits himself to the same missional transformation.

Start with the Destination!

In his expected animated manner, Pastor T delivered a powerful message on Sunday morning at all three worship services. But there was something different. It was his sense of urgency and passion. He cast a vision called "Gold Rush." T used the metaphor of a person panning for gold. He got everyone's attention when he stepped out from behind the pulpit wearing his waders and waving a gold mining pan in the midst of the people attending the service.

His message included four Gold Rush milestones. First, the adventurous effort of finding gold cannot be done without preparation, much like Christians who must receive and understand God's Word. Second, panning for gold cannot be executed from the security of one's living room, like Christians cannot touch the life of a nonbeliever by merely sitting in church and simply absorbing God's Word. Third, panning for gold is a discipline of tediously paying attention to every little piece that glitters in the pan—similar to the Christian recognizing the smallest of opportunities to create a Christian relationship with people outside the church. And finally, successful gold adventurers make an impact because of their diligence and persistence to live their passion every day—just as Christians must take on a life-style of walking their faith every day wherever it might take them.

"Gold Rush" took on a new meaning following T's week of experience with what he saw as opportunity in the community outside the walls of the church. Deciding to launch the transformation to the Great Commission, he announced that he was going to start casting the vision of missional ministry. His intent was to start the process of moving the congregation from their internal frame of reference to external thinking.

Pastor T offered a tender prayer for Todd and his family, emphasizing healing and faith in the face of a difficult time. Pastor caught up with Todd's parents after the second service and was told that Todd's condition had stabilized. The doctors would probably bring him out of the medically induced coma tomorrow. He would more than likely have some memory loss. The question was whether it would be temporary or permanent.

After the services Lil asked her husband if they could dine out before he returned to church for an afternoon Bible study. Lil had a great sense of humor, and T would run with it.

With all his charm, T responded, "Sounds like a date, Lil! If you are going to buy, you get to choose the place." Lil thought for a moment and said, "How about that new restaurant in the downtown area—the Eatery?" T quipped, "I'm hungry—let's go!"

Lil and T had driven separate vehicles that morning, so they hopped in her "Silver Streak," as she affectionately called the gray 2001 compact, and headed to the Eatery. Commenting on her husband's message, she said, "You got their attention today!"

"I hope so! For some reason I cannot get Jesus' command to "Make disciples!" out of my mind. It's our responsibility to live out our faith by making disciples beyond the walls of the church."

Lil asked, "Did last week have anything to do with it?" Without thinking, T said, "Absolutely! Just picturing Leah and all those young people appearing to honor God—"

Lil interrupted, "—you feel they need some guidance?"

"Well, I may learn also. They represent a different generation, and I am not certain the church today is relating to them. Especially when one of my own staff members said, 'They are not like us'!"

Lil clarified T's statement by asking, "You mean that the church is writing them off because they are different?"

Admitting a painful reality, T confided, "Lil, I sometimes think we give lip service to "Come as you are." Are we sending a signal that we are not interested in today's youth?"

"Oh, I think we send that signal to anyone who's a little different. Remember, we tend to think like everyone should be exactly like us."

Smiling at Lil, T said, "You're amazing! That's what I'm thinking and not able to express. Today's perception of church is that of a club. I don't think we send that signal intentionally, but many people outside the church perceive it that way."

Challenging T a bit, Lil requested a solution. "How are you going to change it?"

"You have the answers—you tell me," he said, throwing it right back at Lil.

"Oh, you know my answer. I believe every change happens through relationships."

"Why did I know you would talk about relationships? And that means impacting people inside and outside the church—right?"

Lil came right back with, "Right!—feel better now?"

Laughing, T replied, "Nah, I'm still hungry."

They parked and entered the restaurant to find it very crowded. As they looked over the seating, they saw someone waving them over to a table. T recognized the couple as members of his church.

A friendly voice said, "Pastor, you're welcome to join us if you like." Recognizing Oz, T approached the table with Lil, saying, "Thank you, Oz. It looks like we're fortunate you have two available chairs. Oh, Oz and Ags, this is my wife, Lil. I'm not sure you've met."

"Nice to meet you, Lil. I remember seeing you in church. Lil, this is my wife, Ags. Please, join us."

Oz was a man who worked hard as a truck driver to support his wife and three kids. He often felt put down and left out by society and religion. He and his family attended church on Easter and Christmas to impress on the kids that having ties to God was important. It was safe to say that Oz was a sideline Christian. Although quiet, his wife Ags was very committed to family and was a God-loving person.

Oz explained that the waitress had just brought the menu but they hadn't ordered. "Well, Pastor, how is the God business going?"

Exchanging jabs, T came back with, "Hey, always challenging! To be honest, Oz, I'd feel a lot better if I saw you and your family more involved."

Bothered by T's frank remark, Lil exclaimed, "Do you guys always talk like this to each other?"

"Oh, Oz and I have coffee occasionally and sort of throw jabs at each other. I don't think he's offended."

Oz, laughing, replied, "Not at all! Pastor, I know we could do better with our attendance on Sunday, but I don't feel like your 'do good' church people really welcome us. I'm just a truck driver trying to scratch out a living for me and my family."

Responding more seriously, Pastor stated, "There's nothing wrong with being a truck driver. God gave you those skills and placed you where He feels you can serve Him. Do you believe that God has a purpose for you right where you are?"

"You have to be kidding!" Oz said defiantly. "I think He deserted me and left me with a hopeless future. When I compare myself with those who are living in luxury homes, driving a different car every day, and taking five-day weekends..."

"Oh, honey, it isn't that bad!" Ags attempted to soften Oz's defiance. "We've got a lot to be thankful for."

"I remember feeling that way when I first met Lil. School and survival ate up all the money, and I did wonder if my efforts would ever pay off. You know, Oz, I'm amazed what God has done in our lives. We're not wealthy, but we're happy."

The waitress brought water and took their orders. Placing the orders, Ags and Lil found they both enjoyed fish. The two of them picked up the conversation for a time while the men listened. Eventually their food was served. Ags asked Pastor T to give a blessing, and soon they were involved in a delightful conversation. Pastor was looking for an opening to get back to Oz's comments about church.

"Let me ask you a personal question, Oz. Has God provided for you and your family with the things your family needs?"

Taken aback by the question, Oz paused to think. Then he responded, "Ah, in all honesty I have to say yes. He has provided us with our needs. Financially we are doing all right and actually saving for our kids' education. So far Ags is a full-time homemaker and mother. The mortgage on our house is almost paid, and we don't have any credit card debts. And we've never failed to put food on the table. And before you ask me—yes, I do believe that God is responsible for what we have and that I must be a good steward of those blessings. However, a lot of people have a lot more than we have. Is that fair?"

Pleased, Pastor T said, "First, let me say that I admire your witness that everything comes from God. God has been generous and the fact that you see yourself as a steward of those blessings is a Biblical truth that some people spend a lifetime realizing. You know, Oz, what you perceive as unfair may be Satan trying to deceive you into blaming God instead of thanking God."

As Oz rubbed his graying sideburns, he responded, "Oh, I have at times thought a few bad things of God. Especially when I am dead tired watching that center line at night. I often ask, Why God? Why do You have me in the middle of nowhere at night when everyone else is home with their family, reading stories to their kids and getting a good night of sleep?"

"Honey," Ags interjected, "I know you extend yourself for me and the kids, but what makes you keep doing it?"

"It's strange. Something inside keeps bringing me back to the reality that I am doing this for something greater than me. My family is wonderful, and they celebrate the moment I come in the door from my long over-the-road trips. That welcoming and feeling of being needed makes it worthwhile. Pastor, I suppose you are going to tell me there's something spiritual about that."

"Of course! Oz, I know you were baptized. From that time the Holy Spirit has been a part of your being. Every thought, decision, and action has involved the Holy Spirit trying to guide you to become what God has planned for you. Satan is also working to derail that guidance, but you've remained steadfast."

Oz started to laugh, "That's spooky!" Suddenly he got a serious look on his face and was reminded of something beyond him. "But it does make sense as I think of the many times I wanted to dishonor God but somehow found the strength to say, 'No.' You know—why would God pay attention to me? I believe in what Jesus did for me on the cross, but I haven't been good about going to church. Doesn't God give up on people like me?"

"Oz, why would He give up on you when He created you and has a plan for you? I've no doubt that He set up this conversation we are having today. I believe God is starting to open a door for you to grow in your faith and use the gifts He gave you to build His kingdom."

Embarrassed by the conversation, Oz said, "Come on! You're talking crazy. We just came in here to eat because our kids are at a matinee movie. We had no idea you were going to be here." He pondered for a moment in silence. "Oh, this is beyond me! What you're saying, Pastor, is that God knew and it was no accident that Ags and I are here with you and Lil. Do these things really happen?"

"Oz, don't sell God short," Lil grabbed the opportunity. "He certainly has the power to maneuver each of us to meet today. We only popped in here because I suggested eating out. None of us had any idea that we would have this discussion. Can't you believe that, in some way, God is opening a door for all of us?"

Oz shook his head in disbelief and said, "This is starting to feel like a dream. The supernatural is way beyond my comfort zone. What is even stranger is that I have experienced things like this before and had this feeling that it was beyond a coincidence. I just shrugged it off and continued business as usual. This one is hard for me to disregard. Pastor, you know God better than me. What am I supposed to do with this open door?"

"I don't have the type of answer you want. What's in your heart right now?"

"Oz, it seems like we've had this conversation before," Ags couldn't resist saying. "Honey, what is in your heart?"

"Oh, boy!" Oz confided, "Well, I feel really guilty about not attending church as a family, but it goes deeper than that. You've made it clear to me that I can't compare myself to others. I'm feeling really thankful for my family and also very grateful to God for blessings I simply didn't recognize as blessings." Pausing, he rubbed his sideburns and said, "I'm still confused about God's plan for me. To be honest, Pastor, I really treasure your friendship, and it's been a pleasure meeting you today, Lil. Going to church is something different. I feel like a square peg being forced through a round hole."

"Oz, you and Ags are obviously believers in Christ as your Savior. From what I have observed, you are raising your children with those same values. I don't want church to be considered a round hole that doesn't fit you. At the same time, we must hold true to God's Word. God welcomes everyone, and He made Christ the head of the church. Explain to me what makes you uncomfortable."

"Are sure you want this?" Pausing again, but seeing Pastor waiting for more, Oz continued, "In my terminology, I see the church building as a Country Club made up of people who hold club cards entitling them to gloat about the self-righteous status they hold in God's world. I honestly don't see them serving anybody but themselves.

"In a small way, Ags and I see ourselves as wanting to make a difference in our kids' lives, but also beyond that. We pride ourselves in being good parents and neighbors." He paused, gathering courage. "The moment I step in church, I feel isolated by attitudes and judgment. The service itself is cluttered with man-made rituals that are distracting for me. I guess I'm a simple person who wants the bottom line."

"Thank you, thank you! I admire your honesty. This is serious stuff, Oz, and I guarantee that every word you just expressed is now on my heart."

"Pastor and Lil," Ags confided, "my heart is sad sometimes because we've been members for almost ten years and we don't have one close relationship with anyone in the church. We have to take the blame for not attending, but we also feel like we've been written off as misfits by 'the club.'"

"I can't promise immediate change in everything you've mentioned," replied Pastor T, "but I can promise that you will be contacted soon by some really good Christian leaders in the church who think the way you do. The two of you can help Christ's church more than you can imagine by simply explaining to them how you feel. You have my pledge that you will be in our prayers. I will personally keep in touch to hear about how God is working in your lives."

Half serious and half kidding, Oz asked, "Is this part of God's plan, too?"

"I believe it is! God rarely spells out His detailed plan for us. Instead, He wants us, as believers, to realize that we have unique gifts that He gave us through the Holy Spirit and we should use them to glorify Him and make a difference in building His kingdom." T continued, "He wants us to use these gifts to live out His plan, each of us contributing as He has created us. He's told us that each of us have one or more spiritual gifts, but all have equal value whether it is mercy, hospitality, or leadership.

Each person's use of these gifts is equally important to get His work done."

The conversation was interrupted with, "Ladies, you both had the fish—right?" Lil and Ags nodded as the waitress served their meal. The conversation was more social while they were eating, talking about movies, bowling, and vacations. After they all had completed their meals and were sipping coffee, Lil said,

"You should know that you've made our day. Our heartfelt conversation makes God smile." Placing her hand on Ags' arm, Lil confirmed, "Pastor and I are privileged to be your friends."

Oz was very appreciative as he lowered all his defenses. "This feeling I have is new to me, and I don't know how I'm going to explain it to anyone else. I'm not even sure I know what gifts have been given to me. Our relationship with God is solid, but our relationship to the church is shaky. I know I have to make an effort. We haven't taken communion in a long time. I feel compelled to start there." Ags struggled to keep a tear from rolling down her cheek.

"That's a great start!" Pastor advised, "Maybe you could consider joining a small group also. As part of the group, you can get involved in a serving ministry of your choice. When you find something that feels good and you're doing it for the glory of God and not your own, you have found your spiritual gift and will be living out God's plan."

As they said their good-byes, they all hugged and vowed to stay in touch. In the Silver Streak going back to church, Lil said, "Holy cow, did God send you a response! Oz and Ags represent some of those people you've been concerned about—and it's not just youth. Membership doesn't mean too much if we don't have a Christian relationship with each other."

Taking the opportunity to thank his wife, T responded, "I'm so glad you invited me on this date—thank you, Lil!" Stopping the car at church, he asked, "Lil, will you join me in a thankful prayer before I go to the Bible study? Our Lord is awesome."

"Of course! I'll give you a reprieve—let me pray! And yes, our Lord is awesome. By the way, so are you, T."

Lil's prayer was a thankful and grateful prayer, but she added a petition asking the Holy Spirit to be their navigator to link together a process that would address those who need Christ outside the walls of the church.

As T got out of the car, he said, "See you tonight! Oh, will you call someone on the welcoming team to call on Oz and Ags? Explain the experience we had today and suggest they step up alongside of them and let them know that someone cares. I'll also be in touch with Oz."

"Consider it done! Love ya!"

LOOKING FOR MEANING:

1. What is so significant about the outward thinking Pastor T is attempting to cultivate in his church?

2. With which areas of Oz's thoughts do you agree or disagree?

3. What is the difference between recruitment for your church and T's motive to be missional (introducing Jesus to people)?

Chapter 3—Love God!

"Teacher, which is the greatest commandment in the Law?" Jesus replied: "'Love the Lord your God with all your heart and with all your soul and with all your mind.' This is the first and greatest commandment."
Matthew 22:36–38 *(NIV)*

Knowing about God and knowing God in an intimate relationship are completely different. Jesus commands us to first love God, but He expects that this love is a complete and unconditional relationship with Him.

Chapter 3 finds Pastor T lured into the Village, meeting two young people whom God is placing in the Pastor's life. We begin to feel the challenge Pastor T will be facing in his quest to be missional.

Love God!

The smell of freshly brewed coffee introduced Pastor T to a new day. Lil had prepared breakfast and set the morning paper alongside his plate. T walked into their sunroom in his robe where Lil was waiting for him at the table. With her trademark welcoming smile, Lil greeted him with a "Good morning, Pastor T. Will you join me for breakfast?" Amused and pleased, he responded with, "My love, I'd be honored! You must have something special in mind." They both laughed and sat down as they joined hands in table prayer.

Lil told her husband she knew he would wake up with his motor running this morning. She wanted to give him a relaxing breakfast.

"I presume you have your day, or maybe your week, all planned out."

"That's scary, Lil! You know me all too well. Seriously, what a way to start a week. Thanks, I owe you."

"Of course, you owe me! You will need to be retired with a lot of time when I cash in on all your IOUs. What's your itinerary today?"

"Well, there are a number of things at the office, but I want to check on Todd and then possibly stroll down to the Village, God willing. I feel a connection about something in that Village. I don't know yet what it is. I do know that I want to return and see what God has in mind. The rest of the week is pretty well booked at church. Oh, next week I'm invited to tour a large communications business in the industrial park, and then I have to give a presentation at a career fair at school. Vi asked me to talk about a pastoral career. It's hard to say 'no' to Vi."

Knowing what T was talking about, Lil agreed, "You're right about Vi. I think she is the busiest person in our community and in our church."

Finishing a delightful breakfast with his charming wife, T was on his way in his pickup. He decided to go to the hospital first to check on Todd. He pulled into the parking lot of the hospital and caught the elevator to the fourth floor. The volunteer at the information desk directed him to Todd's room telling him that he was still in an induced coma and there was a visitor in his room. Pastor T walked down the hall expecting to see Todd's mother or father. Much to his surprise, it was Leah.

"Wow, good morning, Leah. I didn't expect to see you here."

"Oh, I've been camping here for about an hour."

Pastor T inquired, "What's the story on Todd? His parents told me yesterday that he would be brought out of the coma today."

"Yeah, that's the plan. I just wanted to spend some quiet time with him. I've never had a friend like Todd before. I don't know if I'm preparing myself for the worst or the best, but the thought of the worst leaves me in a chill."

Pastor asked, "What do you feel would be the worst?"

A little uncomfortable, Leah expressed her concern. "Oh, maybe that he won't remember me, or that we won't be able to share our thoughts and beliefs any more, or possibly that he will be a different person."

"I noticed that you have the Bible opened, Leah."

"Yes, Todd and I would always agree to read something in the Bible, and we'd set time aside during the day to discuss that Scripture. I don't want to disappoint him by not keeping up on my reading. We had agreed to read the book of James. We picked it because we are saved by grace, but I wanted some clarity on the role God plays in motivating a believer to do good works."

"I'm so impressed, Leah. For a person who avoids church, your faith is awesome. How long have you and Todd been..."

Interrupting Pastor, Leah said, "...going together? It's not like that. We are very close, and maybe someday we'll find that kind of relationship. For now, we are friends. That is one of the things we talked about, and we decided not to complicate life right now with any romantic notions. But make no mistake, Todd is my closest friend and I love him."

"I certainly respect that. Leah, your personality and outward display of confidence demonstrates you have it all together. I would venture a guess that you have some goals for your life."

Laughing and brushing her long blond hair out of her eyes, Leah said, "Oh, I don't have it all together. I do have goals, however. I guess God gave me gifts of hospitality and serving—possibly leadership. It thrills me to make people happy or improve their lives in some way. It seems like when I do get involved it also leads to something bigger or deeper, where I am tossed into leading the effort. My career goal is to be a doctor. I should be able to enroll in med school in two years."

"Again, I'm impressed," repeated Pastor T. "I was planning on going to the Village today and hanging out to get a feel of the culture and maybe talking to a few young people. I hope I won't be perceived as an intruder."

Leah expressed that most of the regulars in the Village were quite independent, but loving and caring people. "You'll be welcomed. Is your motive to get more people to come to your church?"

"I really enjoy your candor. The answer is no! If that happens in the process, I will consider it a blessing, but I am not recruiting. My motive is to create relationships and find opportunity to introduce Jesus."

"That's a switch! I thought all pastors were concerned about building their mega churches. Most Village folks I know believe in Jesus. I'm not sure they know the difference between Jesus as a man who did miraculous things and Jesus as their Savior."

"That's my point, Leah. We can know about Jesus, but do we really know Him and understand what Jesus did for us? Leah, have you ever thought about a career in some specialty ministry?"

Throwing both her hands in the air, she replied emphatically, "Never in my wildest dreams! Remember, I avoid church!"

With a smile, T recalled, "Yeah, I remember. Please, just think about it."

Leah responded, "Oh, I have! Not being part of a church affiliation is a problem in that regard. But I have given a lot of thought to serving people with a heart for Christ. You see, Pastor T, I feel I can do that as part of my medical career."

As he leaned forward in his chair, preparing to stand, T stated, "Like I said, you are an intelligent young person who appears to have her priorities in the right place. I yield to your passion. Leah, I can learn a lot from you about the Village culture. Can we continue to talk as a team? If God leads me there, I would be honored to have you mentor me as we introduce Christ, our Savior, to this component of the community."

"Oh, I'd love that. As Todd recovers, I'd like him on board also."

"That's great! Want to join me in prayer asking God to heal Todd with a full recovery?"

"You know the answer to that!" Leah clasped Todd's hand and also Pastor T's while Pastor T prayed a heartfelt prayer.

As Pastor T left the room, he literally ran into Todd's parents. He excused himself for not watching where he was going. They spent a few minutes updating each other on Todd. T said he would call the hospital later in the day to check on Todd.

T rushed to his truck and headed for his office. As he parked in the church lot, he saw Phil, his youth coordinator, leaving the building and walking briskly in the direction of the Village. Pastor T didn't think too much about it because Phil was quite active with the youth in the community and frequently attended functions where he could create new Christian relationships.

Pastor entered the receptionist area on the way to his office. He asked Sue, the administrative assistant, where Phil was going in such a hurry. Sue indicated she wasn't sure but that he had rushed out after receiving a phone call, saying he might be gone for a couple hours.

Sue informed Pastor T that Cole, chairman of the Elders, had rescheduled his appointment for later in the week. That freed up T, and without hesitation he told Sue he was going to head for the Village.

As he strolled toward the Village, he had no idea what he was going to find, but he enjoyed the walk and decided it was time for a cup of coffee. As he arrived, he took a moment to observe the activity in the cobblestoned neighborhood. There were a few artists on the streets displaying their art and a number of young people going in and out of a place called the Coffee Grounds Café. That's where T headed.

As he entered the café he felt a little conspicuous. That feeling subsided quickly as everyone was busy in conversation and seemed unaware that T was a newcomer.

He ordered a cup of coffee at the counter and took his mug to the only table available. At a table near him were four college-age guys making a lot of noise, mostly talking about last night's party at someone's house. Two young women and two young men were talking at another table about their test scores in psychology class. Three young women sitting within listening distance were discussing cute guys. Most of the tables were filled. T spotted one guy with long hair who was by himself and looked as if he were writing the words for a song. He was nodding his head and talking to himself. He would then write something in a notebook. Other than the song writer, everyone T could see was engaged in social behavior.

About the time T felt this was a wasted trip, a man in his early thirties with a crew cut and a trim athletic build bought coffee and started walking toward T's table. The man pointed to the empty chair and asked T if he could join him.

Rising out of his chair, T said, "By all means, please have a seat." Extending his hand, he said, "My name is T." While they shook hands the young man said, "They call me Luke. I've never seen this place so crowded. It must be because of all the homecoming activities on campus. I haven't seen you in here before, T."

T was thrilled that someone would talk to him. T indicated, "That's because it's my first time in the café. I just wandered down here for a cup of coffee. I guess I am curious about what happens in the Village."

"You see just about every type of person. It's kind of a cultural melting pot of the college campus. Sometimes I feel out of place because I'm a little older."

T laughed and said, "Oh, Luke—I envy the thought of being your age. You can imagine how I feel. Do you work at the college or are you a student?"

"Like, both! Currently I am working on my master's degree in communications and serving as an adjunct instructor at the same time. I am also married with a little daughter, so it gets hectic at times. How about you?"

Sipping on his coffee, T replied, "I admire your ambition, Luke. You are a committed person. No, I'm not associated with the college. I'm a pastor of a church just five blocks from the campus."

Luke came off his chair and said, "You've got to be kidding! I'm a 'PK'—a pastor's kid! I don't believe this. Why was this the only seat in the place today? I absolutely never took you for a pastor."

Pushing his glasses up on his nose, T responded, "I think that's a compliment. Are you named after the Apostle Luke?"

"Yes! Yes, I am! My dad said when I came along he knew that I was a unique handiwork of God. He first thought I should be called 'Luther,' after Martin Luther. He and my mother decided on 'Luke' because he was the only Gentile to write any of the books in Scripture. Tell me—you're not really down here in the Village to sip coffee and kill time?"

"Frankly, Luke, I can get along without the coffee, but I have a passion to become more missional in my outreach and also to transform my congregation to be more focused on honoring Jesus' mission. Last week I wandered into the Village for the first time, and it felt as though I was here for a reason."

"Fantastic! Jane, that's my wife, and I did Christian missionary work in Africa for two years. That's before we had little Mary. Since we've been in the states, God's work has been limited to occasional conversations with students here on campus. It's probably more like spiritual counseling. I felt most used by God when I was serving our country in Iraq as a comrade with my fellow soldiers."

Completely engulfed in Luke's enthusiasm, T replied, "You've quite a background. By the way, have you met Todd and Leah on campus?"

"Beyond belief! Todd and I have talked a lot, and he just introduced me to Leah a couple weeks ago. I've been praying for Todd. They are quite a pair. Actually, the two of them were supposed to come to our apartment this week to just hang out and share what God is doing in our lives. How do you know them?"

Realizing this conversation had just launched a new dimension, Pastor told Luke that Todd and his parents were members of his congregation. "I just met Leah in the Village last week and talked with her again this morning in the hospital. They are supposed to bring Todd out of his coma today. So pray that goes well."

Luke said, "I will!" He glanced at the clock on the wall as he rose. "I don't want to be rude, but I have a class in twenty minutes. I'll have to leave. I'd like to visit again. How can I get in touch with you?"

Pastor T handed Luke his card, saying, "The best way to get me is to text me or call me on my cell. This has been great. It's amazing how God intervenes in our lives."

"Thanks," Luke grabbed T's hand with a firm shake, "say 'hi' to Todd and Leah. Tell them Jane and I are praying for them."

Luke placed T's calling card in his wallet and rushed out. T looked around and found some of the younger people were looking at him. It was as though, "If you know Luke, you must be okay!" Pastor T returned his coffee cup to the counter and glanced at his watch. He had a little time before he had to be back to the office. He walked the street and looked in the store windows.

Spotting the young man who was writing in the Coffee Grounds Café, T thought to himself, "I do have some time, but maybe I am getting too bold. This may not work out at all." In spite of that, he found himself inside the book and music store, walking back to the music section looking for a Bible study DVD that someone in the church had mentioned. The young guy was online. T heard a sudden burst of excitement from the direction of the computer as the young person belted out, "That's a blast!" The young man turned around in his chair and saw T staring at him. He said, "Sorry for the outburst, man. It was like I got excited—finding what I was looking for."

Almost at a loss for words, T said, "That's great! Sorry for staring." He paused for a moment before continuing, "You caught my attention. I just saw you at the Coffee Grounds—looked like you were writing a song."

JJ, also known as "2J", was a twenty-three-year-old dude who drifted from one thing to another. He had a band known as the 2J Noise Makers with a few local gigs each month. He had no full-time employment and claimed church catered to women. JJ didn't finish school, but he had a dream of someday having a musical instrument repair business.

The young man responded with excitement in his voice, "Yeah, I'm banging out a song. Hey, dude, are you a musician?"

T felt out of his element but replied, "I can play a little sax, but I have no claim on being a musician. My role is pastor at the church a few blocks from here."

"Man, you're a pastor? Since when do pastors wear jeans and tennis shoes?"

"I guess God didn't give me a dress code, and today I felt like being casual."

"Cool answer—I dig that! It makes you more human. Well, I have to cut out and play with this arrangement for my band."

Compelled to talk to this young man some more, T said, "I take it you are a musician—and have a band too? Before you go, can you give me some advice on some church music? You are at the age of those in our church who are looking for a nontraditional worship experience. You mind helping me?"

"Man, don't ask me—my answers might offend you. I don't do church."

Pastor thought to himself, "T, don't blow it!" What came out of his mouth was, "Try me! By the way my name is T," and he extended his hand.

"Yo, my pleasure, T. They call me JJ. Some call me 2J. Where did you pick up the handle of 'Pastor T'?" inquired JJ. "Is that a church thing?"

"I could ask you the same thing," responded T. "I'll tell you if you promise not to spread it around. Okay?" JJ nodded as the pastor continued, "My dad wanted me to be named after one of the Apostles in the Bible, but he also wanted it to be a lesser-known one. He chose 'Thaddaeus,' who was mentioned in only two of the listings—Matthew 10:3 and Mark 3:18. It never occurred to my dad that my friends wouldn't call me that. As a result, I've been called T since I was a little kid."

"I'm good with T," said JJ, amused by the explanation. "Awesome meeting you." JJ shook hands and started to walk away.

"Wait a minute, 2J—how about that advice I asked for?" JJ looked puzzled as he responded, "You serious, man?"

"Of course I am." Feeling more confident, Pastor T said, "Let's sit down at the table and you can share your taste in music with me. Oh, and I won't be offended by any of your comments. Give it to me as you see it."

"Ya know, this is unreal. A pastor asking me for advice. Is this a lead-in so you can 'save' me from the damnation you preach from your upstairs pulpit?"

"Oh, maybe we will get to that, but I really would like your opinion. I take it you haven't been in church for a while, so tell me what kind of music would attract you."

"I ain't sat in church since maybe third grade. I think I went with a buddy. That was the last time. They ain't got churches for me. Dude, you're cool, but your church music is like—for wimps. I call it women's music cuz it's boring. You know—my kind gets turnt up! It makes me feel alive and jumps out at me."

Compelled to defend the image of women in the church, T said, "It isn't fair to single out women when you talk about wimpy music. Most church music has been composed by men. I can understand you are really turned off by the thought of church. I want to learn more—your perception of music and possibly church in general is intriguing to me. Do you mind talking some more?"

"Sure, dude. I have an hour before band practice. But, y'all can't preach to me about being a phony Christian. Catch it?"

"I catch it! If I start preaching to you, just snap your fingers and I'll know you are being invaded with what I believe. First, 2J, do you believe in God?" Without answering, JJ snapped his fingers. "Wow, you are sensitive about this. Let's try something else. What keeps you away from church?"

Tossing his long, light-brown hair out of his eyes, JJ pondered, "Oh, probably everything. It don't fit my priorities. God can't build my future. That's not my bag. Hey, man—I read this book called *Why Men Hate Going to Church*.[1] I fit the mold that sees women taking over the church—I feel squashed!"

"I'm not sure the two of us read the same book. Yes, most volunteers are women, our Sunday school is dominated by women teachers, and I will admit that the book talked about masculinity being absent from the church, but the book was about how men need a relationship with God and how the church could begin to address that need more effectively. JJ, what are you interested in besides music?"

Looking a bit embarrassed, JJ said, "Oh, you read the book? Man, I never figured a pastor to pick up that cover. Yeah—I thought I'd blow you away. You see, dude, I only read it to justify my staying away from church—I ignored all the God stuff. What do I enjoy? Long walks are cool—nature, camping, rock climbing, sitting around the campfire strumming my guitar. I don't see them in church."

"2J, who do you think created the outdoors that you enjoy so much." JJ snapped his fingers. "Okay, 2J, maybe you will soften later and we can talk about creation. But tell me, if you could change the church, how would you do it?"

JJ sized up T with his eyes and said, "Dude, you ain't gonna like this! I'd tear down all the walls so only the roof is left. Yeah, then those self-proclaimed Christians couldn't hide in their fortress acting like they have it all to themselves. Man, didn't God say something about the Jesus people going out into the streets to tell about Him." T snapped his fingers. JJ smiled and said, "Yeah, ya got me—maybe that's a stupid rule."

Pastor thought for a moment and replied with, "You know, in your way of thinking you are exactly right. Walls create barriers, and the doors and people are not big enough to be welcoming. Are you saying that the church, meaning the Jesus people, should come to your turf and learn more about you and your friends?"

"Man, I don't know! Dude, you rock and you listen to me, but the rest of the Jesus people could care less."

Pastor T felt the beginning of a relationship, but he wanted to know more about JJ. "By the way, besides your band and the outdoors, what do you really want to do with your life?"
Surprised by the question, JJ said, "Y'all really interested?" T nodded his head. "Well, I got this dream of a man cave where I repair musical instruments for people. I'm not so cool with the money as I do something that puts a smile on a face. Dude, I can fix anything you blow into or has strings."

"That's really a serving attitude!"

"You're doing it again—mak'n it religious. I'm not ready for this deep, deep talk. I've got to bounce to band practice. Hey, man, you're an awesome dude."

Not wanting to overstay his welcome, T reacted with, "2J, I want you to know that I really enjoyed our conversation. I'd like to talk again sometime."

JJ responded suspiciously, "Yeah, I bet! I'll be around—maybe we'll bump into each other."

"Say 2J, here is my card with my email address and my cell number. If you have an itch and want to scratch it sometime, get a hold of me. Have a great time with your band tonight."

T watched as JJ left. He thought to himself, "There's more to that kid than meets the eye. I hope we meet again." It was back to the office to clean up some things.

That night T walked in the house dead tired. Lil asked about his day, and he responded with, "Lil, you just will not believe it! God's love is all over the place, and I've been sitting behind my desk for years missing it all. I'll tell you all about it over dinner."

T excitedly mentioned the wisdom Leah displayed, Phil's mysterious interest outside the church, the missional background of Luke, and this kid named JJ. However, most of their conversation was about JJ and T's fascination over the honesty and directness of JJ's approach to life—or maybe it was the challenge that T contemplated.

LOOKING FOR MEANING:

1. What is the value of Leah and Todd reading the same Scripture separately and then discussing what they have read?

2. Why is it that some people might not know the difference between Jesus as a man and Jesus as their Savior?

3. What is your reaction to how JJ justified his response to removing the walls to the church? Can Christians become self-contained?

Chapter 4—Get on Board!

"I was unsure of how to go about this, and felt totally inadequate—I was scared to death, if you want the truth of it—and so nothing I said could have impressed you or anyone else. But the Message came through anyway. God's Spirit and God's power did it, which made it clear that your life of faith is a response to God's power, not to some fancy mental or emotional footwork by me or anyone else."
1 Corinthians 2:3–5 (*Message*)

Our weakness can be a barrier or a benefit. The Apostle Paul in one of his weakest moments found he was nothing on his own, but powerful with God's Spirit.

Chapter 4 presents a realistic picture of the various situations in life that can cause us to resist change and getting out of our comfort zone to serve God and others.

Get on Board!

This was a huge day for Pastor T. He knew that without his staff completely on board with the missional concept, all his efforts would be strictly a solo effort and that would be a disaster. T arrived at the church early to prepare for the weekly staff meeting. "Missional Community" was on the agenda for discussion.

With her normal efficiency, Sue had the agenda in everyone's box the day before and Phil, the youth coordinator, had been reminded to lead the discussion. T was anticipating a little resistance from some staff, so he wanted to feel comfortable that he had done his homework.

Pastor entered the conference room for the staff meeting a few minutes early, and everyone was already there, talking and working on their first cup of coffee.

Phil stood out with his tan from a weekend of sailboarding. He told Pastor T that he was ready to go and asked T if he wanted to set this up.

"Absolutely, Phil. Thank you. Everyone in this room is a follower of Jesus and has a heart for the truth recorded in the Bible. Each of you also knows that in James 3:1 it says, '...we who teach will be judged more strictly' *(NIV)*. We each serve a different Christian vocational role, but what we have in common is the example and leadership we project to the body of Christ and beyond. We are simply held to a higher standard.

"Today's discussion is all about understanding Jesus' missional command to 'Make disciples,' combining James 1:22 reference to serving, '...be doers of the word, and not hearers only...' *(NKJV)*. Pastor continued, "We cannot expect our congregation to be disciples unless we are committed to a process to help make them disciples. Then, and only then, will they be prepared to make more disciples as they, and we, live out our faith in the community. Please contribute to the discussion openly and freely as Phil facilitates. Keep in mind what we are called to do, in our neighborhoods, community, and world. Let's invite God to our table this morning in prayer."

Pastor showed passion as he petitioned God to be in everyone's hearts and guide everyone to do His will. Completing the prayer, T turned over the discussion to Phil.

"Amen! Pastor has painted an excellent picture of what our challenge is today. Let's start by reading Matthew 28:19-20 and Acts 1:8. Matthew refers to what Jesus wants us to do and the Apostle Luke tells where we are to do it. Who will volunteer to read the verses from Matthew and Acts?"

Virg read the Matthew reference: "Therefore go and make disciples of all nations, baptizing them in the name of the Father and of the Son and of the Holy Spirit, and teaching them to obey everything I have commanded you..." *(NIV)*. Phil asked the group what Jesus was telling His disciples and us. "Virg, what is your take on this?"

"I think He is telling us to obey Him by following through on His commands." The lead custodian also had a question: "Excuse me for my stupidity. Is Jesus giving us four commands: Go, make disciples of all nations, baptize them, and teach them?"

"Good question, Virg." Pastor T explained, "What we know of the original script, only one statement is called the imperative: 'Make disciples.' From a grammar perspective, the other commands don't quite match up to the importance of the main verb.[2] We should focus on 'Make disciples' as the primary command. Keep in mind that Jesus' other statements are significant to accomplishing His main mission. Phil, you might want to add to that."

"Just one thing," Phil emphasized, "If we're to make disciples, we can't just sit around. Jesus is saying, 'As you go' or 'Going on our way' or 'Having gone'—Christ's church is not, 'Build a building and they will come.' Rather, as you live your life every day, you are expected to communicate His saving grace wherever you go."

With his head tilted down, peering over his glasses defensively, Jon cleared his throat and started, "Phil, you are absolutely correct, but my role as worship coordinator is to create a meaningful worship environment here at church. I do not see how this discussion even affects me, Phil."

"Jon, you play a huge part in creating a setting for spiritual growth in the worship events you coordinate, but how about those who don't attend or those in the community who haven't heard the promises of Jesus? Don't underestimate your scope of influence beyond planning worship events in the church building."

Still looking at Phil over his glasses, Jon said, "God hasn't given me opportunity. All my acquaintances are Christians. Besides, my life is either spent here at church or with my family."

Pastor was expecting something like this, so he felt he must intervene. "Jon, you are sort of leading us to believe that you feel the Great Commission doesn't apply to you. I really don't think you mean that."

"Of course not!" Jon replied. "I'm no exception. I'm sorry for being such a grump, but worship and music preparation has me up to my ears in work. Can't you appreciate that, Pastor?"

"I can appreciate your demanding work schedule. I'd like to sit down with you and re-evaluate all you have undertaken and see how we can make your ministry more manageable. Jon, would you be receptive to some help?"

"I'd like that! Don't let me hold up the show—maybe we should move on. I'll try to be more positive. And Phil, I apologize."

"Apology accepted but not necessary. How about Acts 1:8?"

Volunteering immediately to read because she felt Phil needed a positive response, Sue took the lead. "I think Acts 1 is the Apostle Luke's account of Jesus after His resurrection entering the locked room where His disciples had gathered. He promises them the Holy Spirit, who would give them the power to carry on His work. Verse 8, 'But you shall receive power when the Holy Spirit has come upon you; and you shall be witnesses to Me in Jerusalem, and in all Judea and Samaria, and to the end of the earth'" *(NKJV).*

Virg validated Sue's response. "My job at church is to be a good steward of the building. I think Jesus is saying my job as a Christian also extends to my family, the neighborhood get-togethers, my woodworking club every Tuesday, my bowling buddies, and even my vacation. We should all share the responsibility to serve God and others wherever we are and wherever we go."

"Excellent example. Lil and I met a married couple a few weeks ago from the state of Maine. Over dinner they told us about their townhouse development where they live and how they responded to help an older disabled woman purchase an electric wheelchair. Everyone in the development association contributed what they felt they could afford, resulting in over a thousand dollars." Pastor said, "When I asked why they did that the response was, 'We saw a need.' Oh, with the extra money they bought her a study Bible, and each Thursday morning they take turns spending time with her in their common goal of reading the entire Bible in one year. They saw a need and showed obedience to Jesus' command."

Sue captured everyone's attention with her infectious smile as she confessed, "When we met last time I made a statement that I have been embarrassed about. I selfishly said that people outside our church membership are not like us. That sounded terrible! This past week I realized that my effort to serve God must go beyond the church office and our members. Because people are not like us, in the sense that we know Jesus, is the very reason we should extend ourselves to create a relationship with them."

"Awesome! What great stuff!" exclaimed Phil. "Tell me, how would you define a missional community?"

"Maybe I can redeem myself here." Jon decided to take a shot at that. "First, I think all of you know that missional is not my comfort zone, but I realize that somehow God will help me with that. To jump on what Virg said, I think one definition is, 'Church leadership must grow the culture of missional attitude where every church member is a Christian influencer in their home, neighborhood, community, and world, 24/7.'"

"Consider yourself redeemed, Jon." Phil continued, "You implied that the church itself, meaning all its members, must grow spiritually so they are equipped to be disciples wherever they go. Thanks, Jon! How about the rest of you: what's your definition of missional?"

"Jon, you hit the bull's-eye. As head pastor, it made me realize that the missional vision of the church should be to Love, Grow, and Serve. More specifically, love God and love others, grow in understanding of God's Word, and use that understanding to serve wherever God takes us."

"I like the word 'grace,'" chimed in Sue. "If I put that in a missional statement, I guess it would go something like this: 'God's gift of salvation is for each believer carrying out the responsibility to share God's message and His saving grace to the world.'"

Virg added, "Well, I get to see a lot vacuuming and sweeping the floors. Someone mentioned we should look for a need. I like that! I think I also heard something about relationships. That makes sense to me, so here is what I jotted down: 'Our missional approach must be simple—allow others to show us their need through trusted relationships and then share our story about living a life with God.' In short, missional is the person we're looking at!"

"That's cool, Virg!" Pastor T was impressed. "Sue, did you get these statements written down?" Sue nodded. "We haven't heard from you, Phil. How do you see missional community?"

"Everyone's statement provides great insight and a real understanding of the Scripture we talked about today. I have nothing written down, but I recently had a situation where I met a young man in his twenties who had attempted suicide by overdosing on sleeping pills. Doctors said they almost lost Kyle. He and I met because a friend of his asked me to visit with Kyle. We met a couple of times and just talked, mostly about him and his past struggles. The man who was killed in Todd's car accident was Kyle's older brother. He feels alone and is having trouble picking up the pieces. He has never had God in his life. I wish I could say that he blames God, but he doesn't even acknowledge there is a God.

"He wasn't talking to me because I'm a Christian. At that time he saw me as this person who would listen. He didn't even know I was associated with a church. In my second meeting with him, he thanked me for listening and told me that he had to work out his messed-up life by himself. He left, and I just sat there. I suppose my mind was telling me to respect his wishes. I hate to admit it, but I also felt relieved that I didn't have to get involved. Kyle was on my mind the entire next day. Finally realizing that God wanted me to come alongside of Kyle and demonstrate Godly love, I started looking for him. Tracking him down wasn't easy, but I finally found him walking near the Village. He was totally surprised but showed that he appreciated my concern for him. We have developed a trusting relationship, but nothing has changed with Kyle's relationship with God.

"I'm pleased that God showed me Kyle's need to want me in his life as a friend. It's also gratifying that he has not tried to hurt himself again. I'm just praying that God will design a path for Kyle to open his heart and allow the power of the Holy Spirit to guide and direct him. I know God's involved because, through Kyle, I have met at least six of his friends who join us periodically in our talks. They are tough kids who reject God, but I'm finding some hope in the type of questions they're asking about the Bible and what it means to have a relationship with God. My trust is in God—that he will show me the way to prepare their hearts. For me, this is an example of missional community. Jon, I pray that someday these young men will be involved in worship opportunities as God fills their hearts and minds with the saving grace of Jesus."

"Wow! Phil, I didn't know that." Pastor felt it was a good time to assign something for next meeting. "Phil's story prompted an idea. Please consider sharing a story at our next staff meeting about a personal missional experience. God doesn't care if it's big or small. Just give us an idea how God's working in your life with a friend, neighbor, or someone you don't even know that well."

Thanking everyone for their participation, Pastor asked Sue to summarize the results of the meeting for distribution to staff and lay leadership. He then called on Jon to close in prayer.

T was pleased with the meeting and felt that staff had a running start on their understanding of missional. He realized that he would have to spend more private time with Jon, mentoring him on the use of his time and searching possibilities for his involvement outside of the corporate worship environment.

As everyone was leaving the meeting, T approached Phil and complimented him on his facilitation. Pastor put his arm on Phil's shoulder and said, "God be with you as you continue to meet with Kyle and his friends. It sounds like a small group to me."

Phil turned and said, "Oh, about that—Pastor, it sounds like you are getting more acquainted in the Village. These kids are all in college and spend time in the Village also. In fact, we usually meet in the park at a picnic table. And Pastor, you have to get with the small-group terminology—college kids call them 'pods.' Kyle labeled our pod the 'Posse.' God has drawn both you and me to the Village. Maybe He knows something we don't."

"Well, that's entirely possible. I have no idea where God is taking us with this, but I know He knows. We just have to be open to God's plan. In some way He will clue us in so we can follow. In the meantime, serve Him and others in a manner pleasing to Him. 'Pods,'— I like that!"

"Late tomorrow afternoon we're meeting again," Phil continued. "I never know who Kyle is inviting. He's taken ownership of the pod. That's probably because he finds comfort being around the 'Posse.' I guess my role is to make sure I'm in attendance. Those attending seem to look to me for discussion leadership. I don't dare disappoint them. Pastor, keep the 'Posse' in your prayers."

"I certainly will, Phil. Keep me updated. Okay?"

Stepping into his office, T was surprised because Jon, who was very independent and rarely wanted to spend time discussing any personal issue, was sitting there. T assumed it was about Jon's behavior at the staff meeting.

"Jon, I didn't expect anyone in my office. Of course, you're always welcome. What's up?" Smiling yet dead serious, Jon inquired, "I'm not sure I have a clue—maybe you can tell me. My lifestyle is very structured and busy. I barely get the things done each day that I'd like. You've seen my office—everything in piles and disorganized. Pastor, that's how my life feels—complete chaos!"

"That's why you reacted at the meeting?"

"Yes, I don't know how to fit anything else in. It's such an overwhelming feeling. Claire, my wife, has a 'honey-do' list for me at home, but it just keeps getting longer and nothing gets done. She's patient, but I know I'm letting her down, too."

Acting as a mentor, T said, "You have a stressful ministry. There is always a deadline. Jon, would you get upset with me if I said that you're your own worst enemy?"

"Do you mean I caused this overwhelming situation?"

Pastor responded, "Not completely, but you do have some latitude to make decisions that would make the things in your life more manageable."

Jon replied, "In my frame of reference right now, it just seems hopeless. After this morning I feel I'm letting you and the rest of the staff down also. I've always prided myself in being able to outwork anyone and doing it with perfection. This strategy is not working anymore."

"There's one of your problems!"

Confused, Jon asked, "What do you mean, Pastor?"

"Perfectionism! That's one issue you must deal with in more moderation. For example, it's great to have everything perfect, but is it necessary? You've carried your perfectionism so far that you don't trust anyone else to do anything. Jon, I've seen your work load increase because you try to do everything. You work with a very competent worship committee, but how much are you empowering them to do?"

"Almost nothing—I figure I'd have to do it over, anyway." Jon paused as though he just thought of something, "Oh, no! I can't believe I just said that. I've turned into a control freak! Nothing's good enough unless I do it."

T smiled. "Exactly! So what are you going to do about it?"

"Well, I'm swamped for the next three weeks, and I'll just have to work harder."

"Wrong answer, Jon!"

"Are you suggesting I should do something right now to lighten my load?"

"Why not? What is the most demanding thing this next week?"

Jon was quick to state, "I know I'll have to spend at least four to five hours designing a cover and getting everything done for the recital booklet."

"Sue would be happy to do it for you."

"But I can do it better."

"Maybe you can. Tell me why it has to be better? And why does it have to be done through your eyes?"

"Pastor, you don't understand: the booklet has to be perfect."

"Why, Jon? And tell me, what is 'perfect' anyway?"

"But Pastor, 'perfect' is when it meets my standards."

"Now we're getting somewhere, Jon, even when you do it, does it meet your standards?"

Sheepishly Jon admitted, "No! I always find something that I wish I had done differently. I'm starting to get your point. My perfectionism is causing more work and worry for me. You are saying that I must learn to use other resources to better manage my work load."

"Yes! Jon, why don't you ask Sue if she will do your recital booklet? It's important you stay out of her face and let her do it her way even though you may have done it differently."

"That's going to be difficult, but I'm desperate. It will save me about five hours. I'll do it—and I'll accept whatever she comes up with."

Pleased with Jon's commitment, Pastor threw his fist in the air. "Great! One more thing—write down five other assignments that you can hand off to others, and let's meet for coffee tomorrow for breakfast. You can explain to me the frustration over not doing these things yourself. Also, consider the relief that you'll experience by focusing on those things that only you can do."

"Pastor, please keep this between you and me for now. It's a major trip in my life, and it may be bumpy. How about 7:30 in my office? I'll clear off a chair and get the coffee."

Laughing loudly, T exclaimed, "That sounds promising! I'll be in your office at 7:30 sharp. I have to be done by 8:15, so have your list ready. Jon, let's bring God into this and ask for His blessing."

They both bowed their heads while T prayed. Jon left. T smiled and looked up, saying, "God, you are so amazing—you set this up!" Pastor T felt as though he just had an out-of-body experience while someone else took over. He knew he couldn't take any credit because most of what he told Jon was beyond his normal realm of logic. Still looking up, he said, "Thank you, God. I'll remember what just came out of my mouth as good advice for me, too."

Sue, standing by Pastor's open door, quietly said, "Pastor, what are you smiling about?"

"Everything, Sue—God is good!"

"I've been standing here for a while, and you looked as though you were on another planet."

"You're right about that, Sue! Did you hear me talking?"

Sue shook her head. "No, and that's a good thing—I'd have been spooked!" Pointing to Pastor's computer, she said, "I just sent you the draft of the meeting notes. Please review them before I send them out.

"That was a good meeting! Change is a little hard for me, so I really appreciate being included. It was a spiritual growth experience for me as well. You gave Phil an opportunity to lead, and he really stepped up. What I'm saying is, 'I really like my job on days like this. Thank you.'"

"You have it all wrong, Sue. I should thank you. God gave you the ability to find order in complete chaos. We all lean on you to keep this place functioning in an organized manner. You contribute so much. Today is the start of a journey God is planning for us. He placed you here to be a major contributor to that journey."

Pleased at Pastor's confidence in her, Sue left Pastor to his work. T went right to the computer and reviewed Sue's report of the meeting. He added a couple comments and sent it back.

His mind drifted again to something he read on leadership. It was the three-step process of change. T recalled the three words: 'Storming,' 'Norming,' and 'Performing.'

He felt the meeting was an opportunity for everyone on staff to storm a little about missional community. There would be more storming, but T felt that there had been a transition toward norming among the staff team. Pastor recalled how Jon stormed rather aggressively but had started to accept missional as a way of life. Norming would take some time because not everyone would jump in at the same time. However, eventually staff would develop a strong bond to embrace the missional concept.

At that point, the staff would say, "I'm glad we came up with this missional idea." When everyone got on board and found comfort in this change, real performance would start to sky rocket. Pastor T knew he had to be patient and allow the Holy Spirit to give each staff person the power to set a missional example.

LOOKING FOR MEANING:

1. What do you find significant in Pastor's emphasis of James 3:1, "...we who teach will be judged more strictly"?

2. In your life, how have you felt overwhelmed and out of control? What did you do about it?

3. Can you think of a situation where change was difficult and the concept of Storming, Norming, and Performing was present in the process?

Chapter 5—Serve!

"Whoever wants to be great must become a servant."
Mark 10:43 (*Message*)

Most of us don't like the image our society has placed on a servant. Human nature indicates that we are more important when we are served. Isn't it ironic that the Bible says that God made us so we could serve God and others?

Chapter 5 brings our role as messenger into the realm of serving. Our Christian characters are starting to learn that the spiritual gifts given to them by the Holy Spirit are to be used as service to God and others.

Serve!

One week passed with Pastor T making some shut-in visits, leading Bible study, preparing Sunday's message, and taking care of administrative things at his church. Pastor T had a productive meeting with Jon about being a good steward of his time. Jon was being responsive and keeping track of his time-wasters before their next meeting. The big one they discussed was procrastination. Todd came out of his coma and was recovering in the hospital. He was having a little trouble with short-term memory and dealing with headaches. The doctors said that both symptoms should disappear. His attitude was good and his parents and Leah were being extremely supportive.

T and Lil also took a couple days to spend some quality time together. They drove to a nearby retreat area and, as pastor put it, "recharged their batteries." It was also humbling for T because Lil was quite an athlete and loved to get T on the tennis court.

Phil was able to deepen his relationship with Kyle and his friends. They continued meeting to just hang out and talk about life things. After his brother's death, Kyle had just turned off the switch and had no interest in anything. Kyle had been insistent that the last thing he wanted was a God who takes away loved ones for no reason.

Pastor T received a text from Luke to confirm a meeting at the Village. Oz and his family were in church on Sunday. He and Ags took communion while their kids participated in Sunday school. T had asked one of the elders to take Oz and Ags under his wing and to introduce them to a few people who engaged them in a conversation about hobbies and interests the family might have. No word from JJ.

T's day started early with "The Disciples" devotional. In an effort to raise up spiritual male leaders in the congregation, the pastor selected fifteen men he mentored for two years as candidates for spiritual leadership in the congregation. Today was part of his weekly one-hour devotional defining spiritual character. In an attempt to get some of his staff involved, Pastor asked Jon to present a brief explanation of Titus 1:8, "but hospitable, a lover of what is good, sober-minded, just, holy, self-controlled," (NKJV).

The coffee was on and everyone was ready to get started on time. Pastor asked Van, a quiet member of the group, to pray. Part of the mentorship was to pray aloud, extemporaneously. Jon jumped right into the Scripture with about a five-minute introduction. It was rewarding to T that the men responded favorably to Jon's presentation. One goal T had stressed was to build up the lay leaders so they could be effective helping the called staff shepherd the flock. Jon followed the familiar format of posing five questions to make the session more interactive. That usually left about ten to fifteen minutes to pray. They knew the routine of splitting into groups of three at the close of each session and each praying what was on his heart. The group then disbursed, going to their various work places.

Van stayed and approached Pastor T about his mentorship. Appearing very nervous, he asked, "Do you think I'll ever be good enough?"

"What do mean?" said T. "Do you think you did something wrong?"

"No! That's not it. I mean that I don't talk as good as most of the men in the group. How will I ever be a good leader?"

T smiled while placing his hand on Van's shoulder. "Remember when we talked about the gifts the Holy Spirit gives each of us when we become a believer? No one gift is more important than the other. What gifts did you identify at that time?"

"Well, I remember being high in faith, serving, and administration."

"That's right!" exclaimed T. "First, your heart's in the right place, you have a strong desire to help others, and you have a special ability to organize and clarify like I have never seen before. There are different types of spiritual leaders. Your humbleness to not take any of the credit and give all glory to God is also your strength."

"Thanks," Van responded. "I'm so honored to be in the group. I don't want to disappoint you or God. Sometimes I'm overwhelmed with the ability of other men to quote Scripture and the vocabulary they use when they pray."

"Van, you may not know the very word of Scripture, but no one will deny that you have an understanding of it. Understanding is the real test. You'll find that God has a way of giving you the means to convey His Word."

"I'm glad you have confidence in me, Pastor. I really do want to be God's messenger in the way I can do it best. I know you have other things to do. Thanks for taking the time."

Pastor T hurried to the conference room, where his staff was just starting to gather for the weekly meeting. He was looking forward to their responses to his assignment of a personal situation where they had opportunity to be missional. After conducting some business items and reports on ministry activities, T said, "Now for the moment we have been waiting for—your missional experience! Who wants to go first?" He saw Sue wanting to talk.

"Pastor, let's hear from Virg first. We took a vote!" Everyone laughed. "Really, Virg has a great story."

T looked at Virg, gesturing that he had the floor. "Fair enough! Virg, let's hear your story."

"Well, Pastor, when you assigned us to be intentional about reaching out to someone, I honestly thought I would end up empty handed. But God made something happen, and all I had to do was muster up the courage.

"Yesterday I bought an ink cartridge for my home printer. At the checkout I paid in cash, receiving a ten-dollar bill as part of my change. I got to the parking lot, and I heard this voice, 'Sir, Sir, you dropped something.' Turning around I saw this high school kid waving some paper money at me. It was a ten-dollar bill.

"This young man said again, 'You dropped this money, sir.' Realizing I had dropped the ten dollars the cashier had given me, I took the money and said, 'Thank you.' The lad turned and starting walking away. 'Wait a minute,' I yelled. I didn't know what I was going to say, but I felt I should say more than 'thank you.' The first thing that came to mind was, 'Why didn't you just keep it for yourself?' He said, 'That wouldn't be honest!'

"My next thought was, 'Hey, he's a believer.' So I asked what church he attended. He said, 'Sorry sir, I don't go to church.' My response was, 'Why not?' He smiled and said, 'Oh, I don't know—I guess it is because my mom is Lutheran and my dad is Catholic. When I was growing up they didn't want to argue in front of me about where to go to church, and it ended up that the best solution was not to go to church at all. If it was good enough for them, it is good enough for me.'

"We had a nice conversation where I mentioned the saving grace of our Lord and Savior, Jesus Christ. I gave him my card and also Phil's card. I encouraged him to contact either of us if he wanted to talk. I offered him five dollars, but he refused. I concluded that nice people don't necessarily know Jesus as their Savior."

"Way to go!" T responded, "Virg, you did good! Sue, we took a vote: you're next."

"I didn't drop money, but my story happened in the vegetable section of the grocery store."

Each staff member related a story that happened the past week in the daily routine of their life. Strangely enough, they all involved some kind of relationship with another individual or group. Pastor was thrilled that they all found satisfaction in their missional encounters. He felt comfortable that God was taking all of them to the next level. In Pastor's mind, the next step was to design an intentional missional process for staff to influence all ministries in the church. He still liked the key words Love, Grow, and Serve as a potential process to prepare his staff, ministries, and congregation to be missional.

T honored his practice of one-hour staff meetings, which gave him time to prepare for his next commitment. It was career week for all the schools in the district, and Pastor T was invited to talk to an assembly of ninth graders about the office of the ministry as a career choice. He drove over to the school. As he hurried in he was greeted by Vi, whose personality was as charming as her long, reddish hair.

Vi prided herself in multi-tasking. She has a full plate with three kids, a husband who was a doctor, and a multitude of volunteer commitments in the community. Vi also worked half days at the middle school as special education teacher, and she and her family attended Pastor T's church.

He had just finished his fifteen-minute talk to the group when he had another opportunity to be missional. Vi and her husband, Tom, were talking at the auditorium door as Pastor T was exiting. Vi was a greeter and host for the resource speakers from the community. She stepped toward T, saying, "Thank you, Pastor, for your involvement in our career assembly. Tom presented just before you. Hey, Tom and I were just going to have a cup of coffee. Will you join us in the faculty lounge?"

"Yes, I'd love to. The two of you are always so busy. It's nice that you can have a moment to enjoy each other."

Rubbing his hand across his bald head, Tom said, "Yes, it is very rare. We both have busy lives and normally meet each other coming and going."

Vi served T and Tom a cup of coffee as they sat at a corner table in the faculty room. "Pastor T, do you take cream or sugar? Tom takes his straight."

"Thank you, Vi. Straight is fine for me, too. Phil is really enjoying your oldest daughter in the youth activities at church. She's quite an organizer."

Tom shared a comment that their oldest daughter was much like her mother. Then Tom's pager went off. "I'm sorry—there's an emergency at the hospital." He shook hands with Pastor T and kissed Vi as he left the room, saying, "Vi, I guess you'll have to host alone. See you tonight."

"Well, that's our life! I sometimes think I keep busy just to maintain my sanity. Tom works long hours."

"I don't know how you do it, Vi. You are a good mother and wife, but you still find time to work and volunteer at church and in the community."

"It has become a way of life. It's a good thing I can juggle several things at the same time. I get a great deal of recognition from volunteering. That keeps me going."

Pastor seemed concerned. "Vi, is that why you volunteer at church—to get recognition?"

"It might seem a little selfish, but I do need recognition because it helps to equalize the identity Tom has in the community. It also helps to establish both of us as part of the shakers and movers who make the decisions. Pastor, do you think I am overdoing it?"

"Don't get me wrong, Vi. Your willingness to get involved is admirable. God wants us to serve others; however, He wants us to do it for His glory and not our own."

"What if I do that when I'm working at church? I still need the recognition from my community involvement. Will that keep God smiling?"

"Vi, you can't just flip a switch and say you're doing it for God's glory. You have to feel it and live it. Besides that, you're trying to negotiate with God."

Stroking her hair and looking at the clock on the wall, Vi exclaimed, "Oh, no! Speaking about flipping a switch, I have to greet the next speaker. Are you going to stick around, Pastor?"

"I can't, Vi. I have an appointment. It was great talking with you and Tom. I feel we may have some more to talk about. Think about this recognition thing. Should it be about you or about God?"

Realizing he had only fifteen minutes before his appointment with Luke, T drove directly to the edge of the Village, parked, and walked about a half a block to the Coffee Grounds Café. As he entered he saw Luke waving him over to an out-of-the-way table.

"Sorry I kept you waiting, Luke."

"Not at all: you're right on time! I just got here a little early. I hope you don't mind, I picked up a cup of coffee for you."

"That's considerate, Luke, thanks. So how is God messing with you today?"

"That's why I called you—God is up to something. Isn't it weird that we met under those crazy circumstances—and that you knew my friends Todd and Leah? I talked to Todd a little today. He's still in the hospital but doing pretty good. Leah had already filled him in on how she met you. Todd said that you are a cool person. By that I think he meant that he admires you as a person and pastor."

"That's nice of him to say. Maybe it's the blow he took to his head in the accident. By the way, did you notice any memory issues with Todd?"

"He does have a little problem recalling some of the things since the accident. I was told that it would gradually get back to normal. Anyway, he was serious about you and your ability to relate to people. When things get better with Todd, is it possible to discuss a campus ministry—possibly using your church as our meeting place?"

"Of course, but I do have a concern. It seems like some of the young people I have met in the Village are not interested in coming to an established church. It may appear that we are just out to recruit them to fill our pews."

"Isn't that the whole point, Pastor?"

"Not really! When I said in our previous conversation that I want to become more missional, I meant I wanted to touch with Jesus the lives of people who are struggling with their faith or have no faith. Many of these people are not ready to join a church—and when they are ready, it doesn't have to be my church, Luke."

"How refreshing—and unselfish also! I'm embarrassed that I didn't catch that. I can see why Todd talked so highly of you. How do you see the concept of missional working?"

"As my wife, Lil, would say, it is all about relationships that eventually lead to a discussion about our Lord and Savior. It's not about me being a pastor. It's about me being interested and concerned about what is happening in the lives of the people I come into contact with. Isn't that called loving each other? When Jesus said, "Go!" he meant "As we go." In that way we are not sitting inside the walls of the church waiting for others to knock on our door. We are among them and part of their lives. From what I have seen in the Village, there is a resistance to organized church but a love for what Jesus offers."

"Pastor, I am amazed at your perspective—and you're right! I have a great deal to learn. For whatever reason, I felt missional only applied to what my wife and I did in Africa. What you're saying is that we are not fully doing our job as followers of Christ if we don't get outside the church and be His disciples every day. That's exactly what Jesus did."

Confirming Luke's statement, Pastor said, "You got it, Luke! Your dad would be proud."

"Yeah, but you had to hit me over the head with it. Being the son of a pastor, it seemed so simple—pray, meditate, prepare, and wow them on Sunday with God's Word."

"What you just said is important, but we get so busy doing church work that we don't make time for the work of the church." Luke responded, "I love it!"

"Luke, will you excuse me a minute? I want to catch someone before he leaves."

T got up from the table and hurried toward the door, saying to someone leaving the café, "Hold up a minute." The person turned around. It was JJ, from the book and music store. Luke watched from the table as T shook his hand and greeted JJ, who seemed puzzled. He said something as he shrugged his shoulders. He smiled and left the café shaking his head as though he didn't completely understand. Pastor T returned to the table.

"Sorry about that. I just met this young man the other day and wanted him to know I hadn't forgotten him."

"Really? You know JJ, too? Give up, Pastor: he's a loner. He doesn't allow anyone to get close to him." T was quick to point out, "Luke, aren't you forgetting God's power?"

"Pastor, what did you say to him?"

"JJ and I met the other day. He found a musical arrangement that he was looking for in the book and music store down the street. I just asked him how it was working out. He said it was a work in progress yet with his band."

"JJ has a band? I thought he was just a street bum. How did you get him to smile?"

"Oh, it's a leftover from when we met. I told him the next time I see him I'll be wearing my tennis shoes again."

Scratching his head, Luke said, "That's weird! I still think you're spinning your wheels trying to convert JJ."

"Luke, you must have been outside playing when your dad was in the shed splitting wood. I will not convert or save JJ—God does that! Remember: relationships! I can only introduce people to Jesus and be there as they're ready to know more about His promises. God works in their mind and heart, and I'm just the messenger."

"Pastor, it's shameful to say, but growing up I took no interest in doctrine. I remember being quite selfish in my faith—like wanting to be a Christian because there were only two alternatives. One was going to heaven and the other was hell. That's a no-brainer. I wanted to go to heaven. Getting back to JJ—Come on, Pastor, not in a million years. He isn't one of us."

"That's the second time I have heard that in the last week—'not one of us'! You mean he's not worth the effort because his background, experiences, and interests are not like a profiled Christian who goes to church every Sunday?"

"Wow! I am really showing my immaturity! No, I want people like JJ to be saved, but it seems like there is so much resistance and so many barriers that we might consider the young people who can be influenced more easily. Forget I said that! How stupid of me. Pastor, will you mentor me? I want to make a difference."

"I'd be honored. Luke, you have the right stuff! I can learn from you also. The first lesson we both can learn is that 'missional' is a process. It is not a program, an event, or an activity. It is also intentional in regard to how we live our Christian lives and how we deal with people who are not exactly like us."

"I am anxious to tell Jane, my wife, about our conversation. At the same time it will be hard to tell her how naïve I am. She probably already knows. I know that she and I will pray about this."

"Tell her I am the one who has benefited by our acquaintance and I look forward to meeting her as well."

"Hey, Pastor—thanks for meeting with me. I have to rush off to another class. Can I give you a call next week?"

"Absolutely, Luke! I'll look forward to that."

With a little time in his schedule, T decided to stop at the hospital for a few visits before going back to his office. He headed for Todd's room first. He found him taking a walk in the hall. Pastor had to get his attention, "Hi, Todd, taking a stroll?"

Turning and looking surprised, Todd said, "Praise the Lord," and gave T a big hug. "I love you, man! I'm finding that my recovery is not a walk in the park. The head injury is one thing, but the rest of my body feels like I got run over by a train. It's good to see you, Pastor."

"You scared us, Todd, but God has a plan. He's not ready to take you yet. Somewhere in this ordeal there is something He's putting together. It looks like you got your wheels back."

"Yeah, but let's go into the lounge. I get tired dragging all these tubes and bags around. It's strange that you say that. I don't know if it's when I was unconscious or in a dream, but I remember thinking, 'Why me?' I suppose I can describe it as anger or frustration about how battered up I felt—I didn't know at the time about someone else getting killed." Todd paused and caught his breath before he could continue.

"Suddenly this feeling of peace came over me. I thought to myself, 'Am I dying?' It was like, 'God, do what is best.' My life was no longer in my control. God must have taken over. It was easy after that. When I came to and saw my parents, my mind was foggy. I could see them like they were far away and their faces were blurred. My first thought as I was trying to figure this out was, God must have decided to bring me back for some reason only he knows about. I was in and out before I really was able to relate to my parents, but as much as my head hurt, this thought was so clear and dominant in my head. Does that make any sense?"

"Of course, Todd. It's comforting to turn your life over to God and see the results of His handiwork. In your case, Todd, He's not done! For right now, concentrate on recovering."

"Thanks! You know, I can't remember exactly what happened except I got hit—like out of nowhere. I am haunted by the death of the other person in the accident. I know it wasn't my fault, but why him and not me?"

"God only knows the answer to that. We certainly feel for this person's family and loved ones. They are asking the same question. Have you had any communication with them?"

"I received a get-well card with some very personal encouragement. He has a family with two children. I can't even imagine how they'll cope with something like this." Todd started crying.

Taking Todd's hands, Pastor said, "Something like this is the hardest thing in life. You almost feel connected to his family. I understand he also has a younger brother who is taking it pretty hard. I am so grateful that God made you with such a loving heart. A lot of people would be wrapped up in only themselves with an unforgiving heart. Knowing Jesus, you know the freedom of forgiveness."

Still sobbing, Todd replied, "Yes, there was never a question that I must forgive. It—it's still hard knowing that these two kids will grow up without their dad. When I saw the faces of my parents as I came in and out of the coma, it was so comforting. I'm so fortunate!"

"Yes, Todd, God blessed you. Your parents have an unconditional love and were at your bedside most of their waking hours. I met Leah, and she was a real warrior in prayer and reading her Bible so she could continue sharing your Scriptural discussions. She shared her love for you by her actions when your condition was critical."

"Oh, yeah! Leah is my strength. What a friend she has been. I love her, too. I look forward to her visit every day. She might not like church, but she is in love with Jesus. Pastor, I know you have things to do. I am doing fine—thanks for the encouragement. Oh, say 'hi' to my friend Luke. He said you met in the Village or someplace."

"Actually, Luke and I had a good talk just before I came up to the hospital. You mind if we pray?"

"Hey, you can't do that without me!" Leah entered the room and all three held hands in a circle and prayed. Todd actually added to Pastor T's prayer and again prayed for the grieving family he was so concerned about.

T visited two more people in the hospital. Then he spent the rest of the time at church with office hours and some other commitments.

That evening Lil asked him about his day. T replied, "It was a busy day, but a great day. I believe God's going to continue making them great. It certainly was better than you wasting me on the tennis courts at our retreat."

Retiring to his study after dinner, coffee in hand, he ran his fingers across the raised symbol of the anchor and treasure chest of the mug his brother had given him. The feel of the anchor reminded him of his brother's unconditional faith in Jesus. The thought of his brother's passionate heart to serve God embedded such a compelling motivation for T. Opening the Bible on his desk that evening, Pastor kept thinking about the events that had taken place and how the Holy Spirit was guiding him into new challenges and a missional journey.

LOOKING FOR *MEANING*:

1. Van's conversation brought out that each of us has different gifts to use for God's work. Does the church sometimes treat some gifts as more important than other gifts? Have you ever felt like God didn't give you any gifts? Or that your gifts were less important than someone else's?

2. Pastor emphasized with Vi that maybe she should re-evaluate her reason for serving. Do we sometimes feel that we are not getting the recognition we deserve for serving God?

3. "JJ isn't one of us!" What does that mean? How come we hear that so often in the church?

Chapter 6—Glorify Whom?

"Therefore receive one another, just as Christ also received us, to the glory of God."
Romans 15:7.(NKJV)

Glorify God! He gave us everything. Just think of our gifts, personality, and passions. Do you really think that we alone are responsible for our achievements? If we honestly look back at our life experiences, we more than likely will have cause to humble ourselves and thank God and glorify God for our life journey.

Chapter 6 causes us to re-evaluate our attitude as Pastor T meets with Vi, Liz, and Phil. His Biblical advice is a compelling message for us as we get wrapped up in the everyday activities in our life.

Glorify Whom?

The next day Pastor T was coming out of the office at church and collided with Vi, the woman from the school career fair, rushing around a corner. She was in her usual hurry to get to her CareNet gathering, where she was in charge of presenting health tips to the group. Papers flew in all directions.

"Oh, excuse me, Pastor." Picking up her papers that had scattered on the floor, Vi explained, "I'm late for my CareNet meeting." As she hurried off, she yelled back at the pastor, "I'll stop in your office later, okay?"

"Okay, Vi—I'll be in until 10:30 this morning." Later in his office, T prayed alone: "Father God, You know all and You have the answers. I come to You for help, Father. I ask for Your wisdom and Your words as I represent You in a sensitive situation. You already know Vi's heart. She's a good person, and I ask that the Holy Spirit work in her and in me as we meet this morning. Guide us both. In Jesus' name, Amen."

There was a knock on Pastor's office door. T looked up from his desk. It was Vi. "You have a minute, Pastor?"

"Hello, Vi. Come on in!" Smiling while Vi was being seated, T told her, "I was just talking with God about you."

"Oh, my goodness, am I in trouble? I didn't know the Big Guy was involved."

"No, Vi—you're not in trouble. I just needed His guidance. What's up?"

"First, I want to apologize for my abruptness at the school. I was just scheduled so tight. It seems like I'm always rushing to the next activity on my calendar."

"Your treadmill seems to be picking up speed. Vi, you seem to be noticing the same thing."

"It's a bittersweet life. I hate it and I love it. Pastor, you sent me into a spin with your comment about doing things for God's glory. I'm embarrassed to say, I never thought of it that way." A tear rolled down her cheek.

"Hey, I didn't intend to make you feel bad. Vi, the fact that you're here right now speaks volumes about your character and your heart. That's what I was talking to God about."

"But I failed God, and I made a fool of myself." Tears streamed from her eyes.

"Love and forgiveness are what God is all about. He knew that we could never be perfect in obedience to Him. That's why Christ gave His life for us. Vi, He has already forgiven you. Now let's work on you forgiving yourself."

"Pastor, I don't like myself very much right now. I understand what you meant in my relationship with God, but I'm still motivated by recognition. I can't let it go. Pastor, is this an addiction?"

"No, there's nothing wrong with you, except that you are an imperfect human like the rest of us. Please realize that Satan works on all of us every day. If he can twist our hearts around and mess us up, he'll celebrate it as a success for him. That's why God is always there for you, Vi. His Holy Spirit works in you to battle the devil all the time. You must understand this and use God's Spirit."

"But Pastor, you're so perfect and you make it sound so simple. I know that God forgives, but why do I feel so guilty and miserable?"

"I'm not perfect! In fact, I fall short of God's expectations every day. I've also had my feelings of guilt. When I was a kid, my brother and I got into a scuffle." T cleared his throat as a check on his emotions. "As we were shoving each other around, I pushed him, causing him to fall off a deck. He ended up paralyzed and to this day, he's in a wheelchair. He forgave me, God forgave me, but it took years for me to forgive myself. Satan still throws it in my face. You are guilty and miserable because you haven't forgiven yourself. Satan is still saying you are not worthy of forgiveness—and you're still believing it."

Vi's mouth dropped at T's story. "Pastor," she paused to regain her composure. "I'm so sorry about your brother's condition. Are the two of you close now?"

"Yes, we are. We talk on the phone frequently and share some pretty deep stuff. He's a pastor also, providing spiritual counseling to disabled veterans. It's okay: the two of us are close—probably because both of us leaned on God. We did a lot of praying individually and together.

"Vi, I feel God is leading us to pray. Can we pray together?"

"Yes, I'd like you to pray, if you don't mind a woman crying. I don't know if I can hold it back. Can I hold your hand for strength?"

"Of course." Vi took a firm hold on Pastor's outstretched hand as he began, "Dear Father in heaven. We know You feel the pain Vi is experiencing right now. We come to You for comfort but also wisdom so we can serve You according to Your will—in Your Son's name, Amen."

"It's a good thing I brought Kleenex with me. Pastor, I'm so sorry," Vi sobbed as she wiped the tears from her eyes. "I realize my heart was in the wrong place and I want to change. I feel stronger right now, but I don't know that I can sustain the feeling that I want to serve out of love for others instead of my benefit."

"The Holy Spirit will give you the strength," assured T. "Please realize that your reward for serving is from God. He's already promised salvation to those who believe in Him. Part of that faith is to love and serve other people. In that way you are serving God—and it doesn't have to be in church. It's wherever you're using your spiritual gift for His glory."

"Pastor T, how do I find my spiritual gift?"

"Vi, I think the Holy Spirit will help you find your gifts. They're unique to you. You've been using organization and multi-tasking skills. God helped you develop those skills, but now that you know you should use them to do God's work, you might find you have the spiritual gift of administration and maybe serving. Concentrate on why you are doing it. God will bless you and your efforts if it's all about God rather than you. Remember, you have not earned that gift or even deserve this gift. God gave it to you for free to serve Him."

"Thank you! Thank you so much, Pastor. I've way too much on my plate. I can't do justice to God unless I evaluate my involvement and focus on building His kingdom with the passion He gave me. By the way, I needed that cry. Things feel better now."

"Vi, you're doing wonderful things for God's people. Just concentrate on the satisfaction you get from knowing that you wouldn't have these gifts without Him. Proclaim His glory and be humble about your own. Now it's I who must leave for a meeting. Thanks for stopping in, Vi. God made this day for you and me."

"Thanks so much, Pastor. And thank you for sharing your story about your brother. It helps me get my life in perspective. I can't wait to share our conversation with Tom."

T was on the move again. He was invited to an open house and tour of a high-profile company in his community. The hi-tech company was expanding broadband services for its world markets. He arrived at the plant and was placed in a group of six people to tour the facility.

After finishing the tour, Pastor T was asked to share his reaction with executive Liz in her office. Liz greeted Pastor with a welcoming handshake and offered him a beverage. Pastor T wasn't expecting this cordial treatment, but he indicated that he'd enjoy a Diet Coke. Liz asked her administrative assistant to bring in two sodas. Motioning for Pastor to sit in one of the leather chairs by the fireplace, Liz sat in the chair opposite T.

Liz had an out-going personality and was a highly paid executive who felt she had earned everything she had accomplished. As a single parent, she lived in an upper-end house in an exclusive neighborhood with her child and live-in nanny. She didn't he felt Christians say one thing and do another. As a result, she didn't belong to a church, although she was brought up in a Christian family. Her sophistication often intimidated people.

T couldn't help but notice the fashionable image Liz portrayed. He felt a little uncomfortable that he hadn't worn a tie. He thought to himself, "Thank goodness I slipped into a sport coat this morning." Liz immediately navigated the conversation to her agenda.

"First, thank you for taking a few minutes to interact about what you saw today. I recognize you from publicity, but until now I have not had the privilege of talking with you. Pastor T, what do you know about broadband technology?"

"Absolutely nothing, except that the technology opens up instant communications all over the world." T took a sip of his Diet Coke and then held up the oddly shaped glass with an etched logo of the company. "Liz, I was expecting to pop open a can. Instead you impress me with extraordinary hospitality."

"Oh, the hospitality is effortless. I really enjoy people and consider it a pleasure to sit here and converse with you. It sounds like you understand more about broadband technology than you give yourself credit for. I have one question. As a minister, how will technology open doors for you to reach more people with your message in the next ten years?"

"Well, in my vocation, it is the message of the Good News of Christ. All believers have been commanded to carry this message wherever they go. To answer your question, I believe technology is something that God allowed to be developed to increase our ability to reach more people and serve Him more effectively. The explosion in technology definitely facilitates endless possibilities for good things to take place all over the world." T stopped talking in anticipation of another question.

"My intuition tells me you are saying that with some reservations."

"You're a very observant person," said T. "I don't want to put down the wonderful things technology has afforded me and everyone else to expand God's kingdom. I feel fortunate to have these interactive capabilities at my disposal and wish to see even more advancements made to global communications. However, it's the moral and ethical issues I struggle with—a proliferation of pornography, abusiveness, disregard of privacy, profanity, and the whole idea that we somehow are above God in our ability to invent the technology." T had the feeling that this sharp executive was already one step ahead of him.

"If I perceive you correctly, you are indicating business has the moral obligation to construct technology responsibly so people don't get harmed. We know that the security of our technology market position has a direct relationship to our ability to remain ahead of our competition. That being the scenario, we don't have time to resolve all the moral issues of the world. What's your response to the complexities we face as an international business?"

T had to decide if he was going to draw a line in the sand. "Maybe that's where we differ. Your comment indicates that you feel your success is completely dependent on your own performance and that you've earned everything you've gained in life—which, by the way, is very impressive."

Liz was feeling a bit challenged. "Of course! How else should I consider my achievements?"

"From a Biblical view, everything we have is from God and everything we accomplish is because of God's plan for us. That places us in a position of managing His graciousness with special care not to hurt but to serve others in a way that honors Him with the gifts He gave us."

"Your Biblical view is extremely idealistic, Pastor, yet compelling. Presumably, I would like to be that person, but my perception of churchgoing people is tarnished by their actions once they get out of your sight."

"Unfortunately, Liz, we are all imperfect and sinful creatures. Sure we have lukewarm Christians, but I pray that they keep working at it and find that they eventually are motivated to be more like Christ. Because I love God, I must work on my sinful nature every day."

"Come on—you're a minister!" Liz disagreed. "I think you're a little better off than most of us on the sin category."

T restrained himself from giving a long answer. "Pastors are human too. Satan tempts us frequently."

"Pastor T, I'm so perplexed. You're advocating that my attitude is completely distorted. Further, that my judgment of others only points back to me and my imperfect qualities."

Liz paused, then continued. "Very few people have ever reversed my conversational focus. Being in control is my expertise—I pride myself in my ability to navigate the conversation to address my agenda. You've been very forthright with me. I appreciate your insight. However, you've managed to tear down the walls of my fortress. That should make me feel uncomfortable, but for some reason I feel secure in confiding in you. May I share something?"

"By all means. You can also trust me that it will not go out of this room."

"I was baptized and brought up in a Christian home," Liz lowered her voice, "but got sidetracked with my career being the most significant thing in my life. After my divorce I completely saturated myself in my work, taking opportunity to be concerned only about my daughter. My anxiety is how all this is affecting her. She has been bestowed all the luxuries of this world, including a personal nanny to make certain she receives the ultimate education. My confession is that I have struggled for the last year knowing that I have kept the love and grace of God from her due to my selfish outlook on life."

"Liz, it took a lot of courage to tell me that. I think you may be a little hard on yourself. I am humbled by your wisdom to cut through all we have talked about and draft such a clear scenario of your parenting and career life."

Sitting back in her chair and raising her hands, Liz responded, "Yes, I'm the person everyone observes as the pillar of clarity because of my vision and laser-focused strategies," she mocked. "Pastor, my security walls just tumbled down! And I feel good about it. I suppose I should feel awful, but I feel so re-energized. Pastor, this interview has been the most productive of the hundreds I have conducted in my career. Can we shelve the technology and just talk about this church dilemma? You must realize this is hard because I have earned a professional reputation as the no-nonsense woman executive who displays no emotion."

Surprised at Liz' about-face, T responded, "Certainly! Are you sure you have the time? With your busy schedule, won't it cause a backlog of appointments?"

"It will, but I will not be at the top of my performance without getting my head and heart straight."

Pastor felt Liz had just handed him the agenda. "Okay—you start!"

"Pastor, I have questions! You made a point earlier that implied corporate innovation should have a moral conscience. Does God expect that I try to change the corporate culture? For example, when we roll out our technical advancements, should we build in controls so the technology does not get used in a damaging way?"

"My comments were very generic in nature." T paused. "But I do feel each of us must act in a Godly manner when we are involved in decision making. Liz, you're an extraordinary person with some skills that are absolutely awesome. It's obvious you have become very successful in a worldly sense; however, have you ever wondered why God created you and what His plan for you is?"

"Are you kidding? Never—at least not until today. You struck a chord inside me when you emphasized our purpose in life as serving each other. Your advice didn't stop there. You stated we must do this in a way that honors God and gives all the credit to God. Frankly, I have treated God as a doormat for a long time in that category."

"What you just paraphrased is profound." Pastor T was in awe. "You're amazing! You must have had a great set of Christian parents, because you are so clear on Christian values. You said your faith has been a doormat since you were a child. Do you believe Jesus died and rose again for you?"

"I don't know what I believe. This really is unsettling!" Liz thought for a moment. "I had it all together—money, position, social status, power. You've made my life appear so empty and incomplete. If I go from being this hard-driving executive to a Jesus advocate, I stand the risk of losing everything." The executive looked the pastor in the eye. "To answer your question, I've never lost my belief in Jesus and what He did for me. I just refused to let it surface with the probability that there was plenty of time for Christ later in my life."

"God isn't asking you to distribute religious flyers to every office as you come to work every day." T continued, "His purpose for you is to do exactly what you are doing, except to do it to serve and honor Him. Liz, as you transition to a serving life at home and at work, the Holy Spirit will guide you to use your skills of wisdom and hospitality. As you rely on the Holy Spirit, you'll find your passion will focus on doing God's work wherever you are."

"The thought of attending church sends me into a tailspin." Liz, for a moment, appeared disoriented. "Do you have a contemporary service? That may be more relevant for me. My daughter, Joey, will really relate to the interaction with other kids. Pastor T, I know I require a magnitude of catching up and it will take more than a sermon every Sunday if I am going to mature spiritually. My first instinct is to dust off my Bible. Finally, my prayer life is nonexistent. My daughter and I can work on that. At this point, I will have to work on recognizing opportunities at work to make a difference. I do want God to be pleased with me."

"Liz, God's already smiling. What a great attitude! Yes, we have a contemporary service and a small-group ministry when you feel ready. Drop in or give me a call if you feel you want to talk. You just made my day!"

As he left the lot of this large company, T's cell phone rang. Ever since the phone call he received about Todd's accident, he'd been a little gun shy about what he might hear when he answered. This time it was Luke.

"Good afternoon, Pastor. I want to apologize."

T asked Luke why he thought he needed to apologize. Luke responded with, "I've been acting as though being a pastor's kid qualifies me to know all the answers. You challenged me yesterday, and I failed miserably."

"Not at all, Luke! Don't beat yourself up. Things we talked about yesterday are a result of pastoral training. I considered our talk a learning experience for both of us."

"Thanks, but I feel pretty inadequate. Pastor, I talked to my dad on the phone last night, telling him how we met and the missional vision you are casting. His comment was, 'Luke, God placed you in the right place at the right time—seize the opportunity to grow as Jesus' disciples did. Then apply your new understanding to build God's kingdom.'"

"Luke, you probably overstated my significance to your dad—but thanks for the confidence. If you're ready and willing, God will take us to the next level. Sounds like your dad would like you to follow in his footsteps and be a pastor."

"Yes, from the time I was born it was an expectation that I should be the third-generation pastor. But it didn't happen, and I have no desire to pursue the office of the ministry. I do, however, want to have a ministry. Trouble is, I suddenly realize that I need you to help me grow to be effective. So what's the next step?"

"I have an idea, Luke. Can we meet next week for lunch—say Wednesday?"

"I can't wait." Luke checked his calendar. "I have a two-hour block of time from 11 a.m. to 1 p.m. Should I invite anyone else?"

"Well, Luke, let me pray about this idea and I'll get back to you with an answer. Can I reach you at the number you're calling from?"

"Yes, it's my cell. I'll wait for your call. See you next Wednesday at the Coffee Grounds."

Returning to the office, T had a busy afternoon awaiting him, including a wedding counseling session, a Bible study, and a planning meeting with a couple of staff members. He was still trying to put the pieces together about the idea he had mentioned to Luke. It was proving to be a problem in that T couldn't get his arms around what God wanted. He would bring it up to his Board of Elders when they met next week.

He was just settling in at his desk when the phone rang. Picking up he noticed the caller ID said it was Tom, Vi's husband. In the instant before he started talking, T thought, "Maybe he thinks I am interfering?"

"Hello, Tom, what can I do for you?"

"It is more my indebtedness to you. I had an unusual lunch today with Vi. She told me about the conversation the two of you had this morning." T was wondering what was coming next. "Thank you, Pastor! Vi has been running on fumes as though she was trying to prove herself as Superwoman. She started a conversation about doing less by choosing those things that make an impact for God and then giving all glory to God. You have no idea the impression you made this morning. I'm delighted."

Somewhat relieved, Pastor T responded, "Vi's very gifted, and whatever she does will benefit from her talents. I prayed that I wouldn't offend her, but I felt she was not receiving the satisfaction she could if she brought God into the picture."

"Again, Pastor, I just wanted to say that I'm grateful—thank you! Vi and I will continue our conversation, and it'll also strengthen our relationship."

T thanked Tom for the call and settled back into his leather office chair, saying, "God is good! Yes, God is good!"

Pastor's phone rang again. He noticed it was Phil. "Hi, Phil—what's up?"

"Pastor, can I stop in for about five minutes?"

"Absolutely, Phil! Now's a good time." T no more than hung up the phone and Phil walked into his office.

"Thanks, Pastor. I just want to update you on Kyle. I also need your advice."

Pastor sensed some urgency in Phil's voice. "You sound pretty concerned."

"Well, I don't know if I screwed up or not. Kyle called me last night about 10 p.m. all upset about something. To use his words, he said he was pissed off at me and insisted I meet him at the pub just outside the Village. When I asked if he'd been drinking, he said, 'Too little to be happy—too much to give a crap.' I told him I'd come if he'd wait for me and not drink any more. I was uncomfortable meeting him in a bar, but my concern for Kyle led me to risk it."

"Phil, are you asking me if it was okay to go to a bar?"

"Sort of—but there's more. There were three squad cars converging on the pub as I pulled into the parking lot. It looked like a war zone with all the sirens and flashing lights. All I could think about was that Kyle had mouthed off to someone and got involved in a fight. Rushing from my car to the pub entrance, I heard something about a gun, blood, and a crazy guy shooting up the place. Just as I got to the entrance, Kyle came out the door. He saw me, grabbed my arm, and said, 'Let's get out of here!'

"My first reaction was relief that Kyle was safe, but as we hurried to my car, I was wondering if I was involved in something I shouldn't be by helping Kyle leave the scene." Phil continued, "We got to the car and Kyle said, 'Peel out, man.' I told him we weren't leaving until he explained what happened."

T noticed Phil gripping the side arms of the chair tightly. Phil proceeded, "Using a few off-color phrases to express himself, Kyle said everything started happening right after he called me. Kyle was visibly shaken and revealed that he thought he was going to die in that bar. Apparently some guy was told by the bartender that he had enough to drink. The guy pulled a gun and started shooting randomly in the room. Kyle said he saw two people get hit. One bullet shattered the booth where Kyle was sitting. That's when he hit the floor like a lot of other patrons. I guess some guys jumped the shooter, disarmed him, and wrestled him to the floor. That's when Kyle heard the police sirens. He decided to run for the door, and that's when he ran into me outside."

T commented, "I remember it being on the news this morning. No one was killed, but about five were treated for wounds. They have the shooter in custody."

"Thank God, no one was killed. Anyway, I convinced Kyle to tell the police that he was in the bar when it happened. They asked him a few questions, and his story was apparently the same one given by other witnesses. By this time the news media was all over the place. We managed to get back to the car without being picked up by one of the cameras."

"Phil, did Kyle ever explain why he was mad at you?"

"Yes, we finally got to that," Phil continued. "Kyle had heard about Todd surviving the accident in which his brother was killed. Somehow Kyle had heard that Todd was a member of our church and I was part of a group praying for Todd. Kyle felt I was somehow taking sides and that I didn't care about his brother. He had this distorted view that I don't 'give a damn' about him or his family.

"He was in no shape to drive, so I drove him to his apartment. We talked in the car until 2:30 a.m. Right now he admittedly hates God, distrusts me, and thinks the church preys on people who are hurting just to get their money.

"Pastor, I did screw up by thinking I could make a difference by myself. Last night Kyle made me feel pretty humble when he said that I perceived myself as a knight in shining armor riding into his life with all the answers. That's when I realized I hadn't partnered with God. I was seeking all the glory."

"Phil, I don't buy that for a second. Maybe in the moment you did think, and even act, like you were some superhero turning wrong into right. Satan has a way of twisting our thinking, but you know you're forgiven. You also know that God just created more opportunity to grow your relationship with Kyle."

"I may have blown that!" Phil leaned forward and placed both hands on Pastor's desk. "In the heat of the discussion with Kyle I told him that he had a choice. He could either remain mad at the world, blaming everyone else for what happens, or start realizing that God is a shared party in our relationship. And that we should spend time sharing our feelings and experiences until we figure out what God has in mind."

Concerned by Phil's stressed body language, T inquired, "What was his reaction?"

"Pastor, my statement angered him. With a few choice words, he told me to mind my own business and slammed the car door as he staggered to his apartment." Phil sighed, "I haven't heard a word from Kyle. I've been praying he would call me, but—nothing."

"Phil, do you mind if we both pray—right now?" Together they prayed for guidance, Kyle's welfare, and the victims of the shooting.

"Thanks, Pastor! Oh, about going to the pub..."

"Hey, Phil, I would have done the same thing. God bless you for your courage. Kyle will realize that you have his best interest in your heart. He may need some time to process what happened last night, and God will help with that."

Phil left, and Pastor T sat at his desk reviewing the experience Phil had shared. In the series of bad events, Pastor was convinced that God would lead Phil and Kyle to mend their relationship. T felt confident that Phil would have a Christian influence on Kyle and other young people because of his love for God and his loving passion for other people.

After finishing things at the office that afternoon, Pastor T headed home feeling lifted by God's work in his life. He had a lot to tell Lil.

LOOKING FOR MEANING:

1. Pastor T told Liz that because God gave us everything, we have the responsibility to manage His graciousness with special care not to hurt but to serve others. How do you relate this statement to stewardship as it is practiced in the church?

2. How do you feel about corporate America displaying a moral conscience?

3. How can we do exactly what we do each day, but in such a way to serve and honor God?

Chapter 7—Love Each Other!

"...Love one another. In the same way I loved you, you love one another. This is how everyone will recognize that you are my disciples—when they see the love you have for each other."
John 13:34–35 *(Message)*

Love each other! As Jesus was preparing to leave the twelve disciples He wanted to emphasize His expectations. His message was that love is to serve as the distinguishing feature of discipleship.

Chapter 7 makes us think how we can create Christian relationships without being threatening to the other party.

Love Each Other!

Well, it was another early meeting for Pastor T. Three men from the Disciples Group were planning a servanthood event as part of their two-year journey with Pastor T. As they sat in a riverside café eating breakfast, they enjoyed the open-air patio and the terrific view. Van, who had talked to T about his speaking ability, was in attendance along with two other men from the Disciples Group. Pastor T took the lead.

"Van, you are the super-organized person of the group. Will you please chair our meeting today and keep us on track?"

"I guess I can handle that if you guys help me out. First, let's talk about the end result so we know our destination. Pastor, can you start by telling us what you see as the goal for this serving process we are to come up with for the group?"

"Hey, I like your approach, Van. I've emphasized to all of you for the last year of your disciple mentorship that we should think, talk, and act more like Jesus. Well, Jesus was all over the place with His ministry—by the lake, on the lake, in the hills, north, south, and in the streets.

"The first part of my goal is to get outside the walls of the church and impact new people. Jesus always had one goal in mind. That was to teach, through whatever means, so people would know Him and why His Father placed Him on this earth. Putting that in our language today, it means that our goal should be to build God's kingdom with people beyond the walls of the church whose lives do not include the knowledge or understanding of Christ."

Mick, a flooring contractor of ten years, asked Van, "Why outside the church?"

"We tend to be a congregation that feels church is something we come to, but let's not forget the church is people who should go out and touch the lives of those in our neighborhood, community, region, and the world. Pastor, help me out here."

"Well put, Van! That's it exactly. The whole purpose of Christ's church is to reach people who don't know Christ as their Lord and Savior."

The other disciple was an investment broker named Dan. "Good, we know where we have to accomplish our goal. Does anyone have a suggestion as to what our project should be?"

Van felt strongly about the concept of process. "One comment from my perspective is that we should not be looking for a one-time project or event but maybe an on-going process."

Dan couldn't resist. "What do you mean, Van—'process'?"

"Well, I'm not that good with words, but an event is conducted and it's over—and we stop doing. A process is on-going and never ends and is a building block to the end goal. Process has more long-term clout. We already know Jesus' three-year journey with His disciples was a planned process, not a project or event."

"In my flooring business, it's a constantly changing process because of new techniques and materials." Looking at Pastor T, Mick jokingly said, "That's going to be tough. Maybe we should have a kids' church on the playground every Saturday—just kidding, guys!"

"Wait a minute—that's a great idea, but with a different twist. I haven't filled the three of you in on my experience in the Village with young people yet." Pastor T went into an explanation of the opportunity for a Village ministry and the relationships he has been building.

"I know from my financial business that relationships lead to unbelievable opportunities, but Pastor, when do you find the time? And you, Van, you're the idea man—what have you got?"

"Hey, guys, I don't know if this will work, but I own a building in the Village, and I just use it for storage right now. Is that something we could fit into this puzzle for a meeting place? Pastor, do you see any potential?"

"Fantastic! You guys just identified a process I didn't even know existed until now. Listen, if the three of you are willing, I'm having lunch next week with a young man who is looking for a ministry in the Village. Are you guys ready for lunch next Wednesday?"

Dan asked, "What are you talking about?" But Van was tuned into Pastor's thinking: "I think Pastor T is combining two or three things that might help young people and at the same time provide us with a servanthood process. Plus our market segmentation, in a marketing sense, is the Village patronage."

Still foggy on the discussion, Mick asked, "Is the point to convince them to join our church, Pastor?"

"No! Nothing like that! Our goal is to provide an informal setting for young people to get to know and understand Jesus—then to use this knowledge to serve others. Joining our church is not the goal! You see, many of these young people know something about Jesus but feel the formal church is a club-like institution that judges people on the outside. Choosing to join our church or any other church will be a possibility and a blessing, but it will not be our immediate focus."

Van felt confident that pieces would come together, but he wanted to clarify the purpose of the meeting. "It seems like we have a lot of loose ends. Are you suggesting, Pastor, that we attend this luncheon meeting and smooth out the edges to this concept? I'm guessing that you feel it'll all come together at that meeting."

"Again, well stated, Van. I'm not even sure what the concept looks like yet. However, with all of us in prayer and thinking about what could be, God will lead us exactly to where He wants us. My new contact in the Village is the son of a Christian pastor. He and his friends just might fill in some of the blanks to an exciting serving opportunity for our Disciples Group." T handed out a couple pages for each of them to read on missional church.

Everyone agreed to attend the meeting and pray for an outcome that would be pleasing to God. T left and headed back to church, where he had an adult baptism scheduled. He also wanted to piece together an outline for his message on Sunday. He arrived at church about forty-five minutes before the baptism, giving him opportunity to formulate his message outline.

T immediately started working out what he might say on Sunday. It was okay, but he still had all these things about the Village floating around in his head. He decided to stroll down to the Village after the baptism. Pastor had no idea what for, but he felt it might bring clarity to create a winning combination for his Disciples Group and the young people in the Village. At this point, T wasn't even certain how the Disciples would contribute to this ministry.

Pastor T spent some time preparing the baptism family and conducted the sacrament in the church. He thought of a few more ideas for his message, so he returned to his office.

He finished the outline for his Sunday worship message. He then walked the five blocks to the Coffee Grounds in the Village with his outline in hand. It was a beautiful day, so T sat by the window overlooking the sidewalk mall to enjoy God's handiwork. Young people were starting to recognize him with a nod or "How you doing?" After a few minutes of tenderly sipping his hot coffee, he saw JJ walking past the window.

Pastor T tapped on the window to get his attention. JJ turned, recognized who it was, and gave two thumbs-up. T motioned to JJ to come in and join him. JJ looked at the time and walked into the café. "Hey, 2J, it is great to see you. It's been a while since we've had a real conversation."

"Yeah, man. I guess so. It looks like you got your line out trolling the streets for the unsaved again."

"Whenever I get a chance, 2J." They butted fists to greet each other and sat down. "Tell me how your band is going and have you thought any more about your music instrument repair business?"

"Band's awesome, and I dream all the time about my mancave business." Stroking his long hair, he said, "I thought we saw the last of each other. I still have your card, but I shook off our meeting as a one-time thing. You can't be that interested in a music bum like me."

"Oh, I'm interested in you all right! Your honesty and outlook intrigues me. Besides that, you have a likeable personality."

"Dude, I'm too street smart to swallow those compliments. You use honey on your hook. Well, Pastor Dude, what are you doing here? Shouldn't you be at the church sprinkling water on someone?"

"You know, 2J, I did have a baptism this morning. This time it was an adult person who felt moved to be accepted into God's holy family. I just took a break to review the outline for Sunday's message and start getting my thoughts together while I enjoyed the beautiful day. You know, JJ, God did make everything we see!"

"Man, you never give up! I won't snap my fingers this time; anyway, the snapping thing was your idea. What you mean—you baptized an adult? Isn't that just for babies? Give me the short version so I don't have to listen to your sermon."

"Yes! And no!" JJ was amused. Laughing, he said, "That's short—I love it! I'll give you some slack—I thought all your people were sprinkled right after they were born."

"Generally that's true in our church, but some people don't have the advantage of knowing Jesus until they are older. We believe that baptism is the means by which believers are placed into the body of Christ."

"That's spooky! Dude, you mean we take a different body?"

"Not literally. The body of Christ I am referring to is God's family, or the people in the church. Jesus is the head of the church. We could say the family of Christ."

"I remember that dude on the cross. I saw the movie *Passion of the Christ*.[3] There was another bad dude on the cross next to Him who said something like 'Remember me when you go to heaven.' Didn't the Jesus guy say that the criminal would go with Him to heaven? The criminal dude wasn't baptized, was he?"

"You have a couple questions, JJ. First, you're correct. There were two convicted criminals crucified with Jesus. One of them did acknowledge that he believed in Christ as God, and Jesus responded with, '...today you will be with Me in Paradise,' Luke 23:43 (*NKJV*). Secondly, the dude—I mean the criminal—was not baptized, at least in the sense of baptism with water. This would indicate that you can be saved through faith and repentance without being baptized. JJ, are you softening on me a little bit?"

JJ chuckled but then got serious, "Chill out! That's all in the Bible?"

"Yes, and much more. It is the greatest book on life that you can study."

"I never had a Bible and never really wanted one. Growing up in the streets I had to live by my own bible."

"Tell me, 2J, what was the most important lesson you learned on the streets?"

"I needed someone I could trust—who would cover my back. I had this friend who knew more about gangs and life than I did. He taught me how to survive. He got killed about three years ago in a stupid fight with some of the street bullies. He violated his own rule—never battle alone! He told me and another guy to run while he tried to settle this war himself."

"I'm sorry for your loss. He sounds like a good friend. That's kind of what Jesus did. He died for our sins so we could be saved. By His grace we are able to be forgiven our sins. Another thing: your friend was right. Never battle alone! You were talking about some senseless fight, but I'm talking about a fight we have every day with Satan. He works on us so hard, we couldn't possibly survive without faith in our Savior, Jesus Christ. We also need one another, as Christians, in a sinful world."

"Dude, you confuse me with your faith talk! But, you know, man, you are the only person I have really talked to since my friend died. I don't buy into your scheme of church, but I do relate to feeling like I want to belong to something bigger than me. As dangerous as it was on the streets, I always felt I could depend on my friend. Since the funeral, I retreated from the streets and earned enough to have a small basement apartment and tried to do music to occupy my time."

"You know what, 2J? Your story is so compelling I'd like to use it in my message on Sunday. Will you give me permission to do that?"

"I thought you had your thing prepared for Sunday?"

"Yes, I did," T said as he crumpled his sermon outline. "But our conversation is real. It's something my congregation should hear."

"Yeah, I guess so. Don't use my name. And another thing, dude, you are not sucking me into attending church just because you are going to talk about me. You're sort of crazy. My story is nothing special."

"Oh, but it is! And JJ, you are special. Anything God creates is special, and He never loses interest in His children."

"Come on—get real! You make it sound like God's my father. I lost my mom and dad in a car accident when I was eight years old. That's when I went to the streets. My best home after that was a cardboard box."

"Wow, you have experienced conditions I can't even imagine. I can understand that you don't trust me because I represent a completely different way of life. But God's your heavenly Father as He is mine. He knew you before you were born, and He knows of your experiences on the streets."

"Dude, that's even more reason not to trust God. Why'd He let my parents die, and why'd I have to freeze, go dirty, and be hungry on the streets? A father should take care of His kids—right?"

"JJ, that is the most difficult question to answer. God did not desert you, even though you may feel like He did. He does tell us in the Bible that our life will have trials. But He allows this to happen out of love so we can grow stronger in our faith and develop a closer relationship with Him. I really believe He has brought you to a crossroad in your life. You can choose to serve Him, or you can wander aimlessly without finding the joys of having that relationship with God."

"That's bottom-line stuff! I dig that, but I'm in way over my head with you and your 'serving God,' 'relationship with God,' and 'Father-in-heaven stuff.' I'm so screwed up. I lived in a world that gave me nothing, man. I stole it, fought for it, or went without. You're telling me I can be forgiven and it's free? That don't make sense to me. Man, you're tippin' my world upside down."

"JJ, the most important thing to me right now is that you and I find some common ground so God can come into your life. Don't worry about attending church right now. Our meetings are a form of worship. I do want to pray for you and eventually pray with you. Nothing is more important to me than your friendship and for you to accept the fact that God wants you back. God is reaching out to you right now!"

"Pastor Dude, you can't make a tough kid cry, but I have to admit you make me feel warm inside. I like the feeling. Remember, Pastor Dude, I'm not committing to anything, but I'd like you as a friend."

"Would you be willing to meet a small number of people I know? These people are all struggling a little with things in their life, and I think you can help them and yourself at the same time. I'll be there also and make sure we keep the conversation within your comfort zone."

"Man, you don't give up! I'd normally laugh in your face and get some distance between us. I trust you—a little. So let me think about it."

"JJ, can we set up a time to meet next week right here for breakfast. My treat!"

"Now, dude, you are buying me." Laughing, JJ added, "I'm not for sale! Hey, man, if you want to spend your money, I can't pass it up. I'll put Friday at ten on my calendar." JJ laughed as he wrote it on his hand.

"At breakfast, I want to hear about your plan for a music repair store. Let's call it your business plan."

"What's the point? I don't have any money and a place I can start a business."

"Don't count God out on that one, either. Just do your homework!"

"You have something up your sleeve. Dude, what strings are you going to tie to this? You are not getting me in church! Keep it up, and I might bail."

"Trust, JJ, trust! See you next Friday. Think about meeting with the other people I talked about."

As Pastor T walked back to the church, he couldn't help himself. He repeatedly clenched his fist and pumped his arm, saying, "Yes, yes, God! Thank you, God!" He was almost walking on air from the feeling he had following his conversation with JJ. He felt God's power working as his relationship with JJ jumped to the next level. T thanked God for the love he felt toward JJ. He just knew that there was still a bigger plan, and JJ was going to somehow emerge as a Christ-centered discipleship leader. "It's a matter of time," he thought.

The events of the day had changed the scope of the meeting with Luke. About halfway back to the church, T punched Luke's number into his cell. Luke picked up, saying, "Pastor, what can I do for you?"

"Hey, Luke, that idea I want to discuss with you just got bigger—God's working overtime."

"Great! I can't wait! Pastor, are we still on for Wednesday noon?"

"Yes, absolutely! Just a slight change. I'm bringing three of my disciple apprentices who I met with this morning. I want them to meet you and a couple of your friends so we can talk about this idea. I believe God will produce a synergy that will take us there."

Trying to get some answers, Luke asked, "Take us where?"

"Where He wants us to go! What He intends for us to do! Who He wants us to impact with Christian relationships and His Word! Luke, can you invite two people you feel can contribute to this vision?"

"What vision? Pastor, you are totally unconventional. What was the question? Yes, of course, I'll invite two more. Did you know Todd is out of the hospital? He and I went for a short walk this afternoon. He said he was a little weak, but he's supposed to increase his exercise each day and not just stay in the house. It might be too much for him to attend, but I want him in the loop. I'll see what I can do."

"Hey, Luke, with the possibility of seven of us, we should have a little privacy. Any ideas?"

"Yes, I'll take care of it right away. The Coffee Grounds Café has a meeting room I can reserve for tomorrow. Consider it done!"

"I knew you'd come through. See you Wednesday. God bless!"

It was back to church to revise Sunday's message. Opening the door to his office, T saw a note on his desk from Sue marked "Important." His first thought was that something had happened requiring him to shift into urgent gear. He unfolded the note and found it was from Lil. She had invited the visiting missionary and his wife over for dinner that night and asked T to be home by 6 p.m. There was a smiling face drawn on the note. Lil said she checked with his assistant, and his calendar was clear. It was signed, "The Boss!"

Smiling and enjoying the moment, T realized he only had a couple of hours. He made good use of his time and headed home. T started thinking about the dinner conversation with the missionary couple. She was born in China, and he was born in the United States. They met at an international youth rally in China about fifteen years ago. After courting for five years and studying Christian beliefs, they were both baptized and eventually married in a Christian church.

Walking through the door of his house, T noticed that there were two pair of shoes neatly placed in the entry way. T never took off his shoes because he usually had holes in his socks. This time he removed his shoes—fortunately, no holes. Lil took charge and ushered T into the formal living room and took care of the introductions. The East Asian couple both stood and nodded with a little bow. As T motioned for the couple to sit down, he said that he was honored they could accept the invitation. Lil went back to the kitchen and took a casserole out of the oven. After about five minutes she returned and invited them to come into the dining room to eat.

Pastor offered the blessing and made sure that the guests were served before he started any conversation. They spoke mainly about the China ministry and the challenges facing them in that culture. One thing kept ringing in T's head: conversion to Christian beliefs must come through relationships and a nonthreatening environment. Thinking of JJ and the other young people in the Village, T was convinced that his church building would be of no immediate value in the transformation of these young people. They needed to establish a relationship to a Christian influence, and it would have to be done on their turf.

He also realized that his missionary friends had opened another door for short-term mission work. He realized God was opening his eyes to opportunities. Pastor was excited about all the missional things that were literally coming out of the woodwork. However, at this point, he wasn't capable of assembling all these pieces into a missional effort he and his congregation could manage. He knew God would lead him to a workable plan.

It was a great evening. Lil's vegetable casserole was a fine choice, as it turned out their guests didn't eat red meat. After the couple left, Lil asked T where his mind had been during the dinner conversation. She felt he was processing many things that were said about the China ministry into his own backyard. A little paranoid, T asked if he appeared rude. Lil said, "Absolutely not, but I know you pretty good."

Lil encouraged T to talk to her about his day and how his plan was coming together. After an hour of kicking things back and forth, they decided they had better clear the table and do the dishes.

LOOKING FOR MEANING:

1. Explain the type of relationship you see developing between Pastor T and JJ.

2. As Christians, why do we need each other?

3. Pastor T was listening to the missionary couple talk about adjusting to the culture. Why is this step important in developing relationships?

LOOKING FOR MEANING

1. Explain then do credit unions you see developed between cells 1 and 3?

2. As Christians, why do we need each other?

3. Protect was taught that misconceptions exist from requiring close living. Why should important relationships important?

100

Chapter 8—Called!

"When morning came, he called his disciples to him and chose twelve of them, whom he also designated apostles..."
Luke 6:13 *(NIV)*

Christ had many disciples. On this occasion, He called twelve as the "sent ones" and commissioned them as Apostles with special authority to deliver His message, discipleship.

Chapter 8 is a reminder that when we find ourselves in situations to advance God's kingdom, we may be "called" by God to use those gifts he gave us to glorify Him.

Called!

Birds outside of T's bedroom window were extra loud that morning. It didn't matter, because pastor had been awake since 4:30 a.m. He was anxious to face the opportunities of the day: it was Wednesday, and the meeting he had scheduled with his Disciples Group and the Village young people was foremost in his mind.

As he lay in bed looking out the window at another beautiful day, he asked himself, "What would Jesus be thinking right now? Would He be praying? Would He be thanking God the Father? Would He already know the results of the day? Would He be excited about another day to serve His Father's will? Would he be concerned about His people?" The answer was probably "yes" to each of these statements.

T realized that not knowing how things were going to turn out was most unsettling and, at the same time, most motivating. His faith was projected in his comment to Lil, as she was now awake also. "Lil, this is going to be God's day to take us all by the hand to generate His ministry." Yawning and stretching her arms, Lil said, "Amen to that!"

After breakfast T received a call on his cell from Van. Pastor picked up and said, "Good morning, Van! Couldn't you sleep either?"

"Actually I slept pretty well, but I did wake up early thinking about our meeting. First, thank you for showing me that leadership is more than talking. I appreciate the confidence you had by asking me to chair the meeting the other day. Secondly, I've been praying that God will give us wisdom and guide us to put the pieces together today. Is there anything you want me to prepare for the meeting?" He laughed: "You know I don't like surprises!"

"Thanks for praying—that speaks volumes of your character. Did you read the literature I handed out on the missional church?"

"Yes, I did. Missional is much clearer to me now, and I can see why you are so passionate about moving our congregation in that direction."

"Van, would you feel comfortable giving a short explanation of 'a missional church' at the meeting?"

"If you don't mind me stumbling through it, I'll put something together, Pastor."

"I know you'll be organized and do a good job. I'll see you at the meeting."

Pastor T was in a hurry to get to the office so he could read his Bible and meditate on the noon meeting. He could feel the pressure mounting because he knew that everyone would be expecting a solution or something astounding from him. Instead, he'd be asking them to share their thoughts and visions. From that, with God's help, he was confident someone or multiple people could take the pieces and design the ministry concept. He also wanted everyone to take ownership and be a stakeholder in the process. If it were his idea alone, he knew it would not be successful. In addition, everyone had to feel God's hand in this collaboration.

T had a meeting scheduled to review Jon's progress on organization and management of his time. Jon was making good progress, especially on the acceptance of the missional concept. Procrastination was still his biggest hurdle.

It was late morning, and T received a phone call. It was Todd. "Good morning, Todd. How are you doing?"

Sounding upbeat, Todd said, "Probably better than the doctors expected. I'm home and gradually getting my strength back."

"Todd, how about the headaches and memory?"

"Yeah, still some headaches, but getting less intense. What's the other question?" He laughed. "Just kidding! My memory's okay except for a period of time after the accident and until I was on my way to the hospital. Anyway, the reason I called is because Luke called and told me about the meeting today in the Village."

Pastor asked, "Are you able to come?"

"I want to, but it might be a little much. Can you mention at the meeting that I'm on board? Luke was a little vague and said that you have something up your sleeve. He meant that in a good way."

"No hidden magic, Todd. I do expect that God will somehow inspire us to come up with the start of a workable plan today."

Todd was a little hesitant, but he had some thoughts about the Village, "Pastor, if I may suggest something—"

"Let's hear it, Todd!"

Clearing his throat, he began, "Well, a lot of the people my age that frequent the Village are artistic. They play guitar, paint, read poetry, do stained glass, fabric art, etc. The other thing is they seem to enjoy people. There might be a way to use those traits to parallel a spiritual growth ministry."

"Todd, are you suggesting we use their interest in the artsy stuff to create the gathering so there is an appreciation of each other's talents? You know, Todd," T said with excitement in his voice, "we can spin off of that with discussion of how God works in their lives."

"I don't think we have to be subtle about our ministry, but if they come to realize that they can glorify God through their artistic ability, they may respond to Jesus and His love a little easier."

"I'm on it! Todd, that's a great idea. I'd like to start our discussion with that today. You don't mind, do you?"

"Not at all. I wish I could be there."

"You'll be missed today, but it's wonderful that you will be involved soon. The one thing I have to bring to life in the Village ministry is a group of disciples from my church that I want involved supporting this outreach. Any ideas, Todd?"

"The Village folks will probably not like a lot of structure and certainly not church traditions. But they like to hang out. Age is not a factor. Maybe your disciples could trade off acting as hosts just to make sure new people get introduced and feel comfortable. They also like to munch on something with a soft drink or even water in their hand. Maybe your disciples could— enough! I'm getting carried away. Thanks for your time, Pastor. Break a leg!"

"Thanks, Todd! I'll keep you in the loop."

As T sat back in his office chair, he raised both hands, looked up, and said aloud, "Manna from heaven. Thank you, God. What great ideas." Looking at his watch, he realized he had only twenty minutes. He made his exit and headed straight for the Village with a clipboard in his hand.

As he entered the Coffee Grounds Café, he immediately saw Luke motioning him to the back room. It was just the two of them. T decided to order a pot of coffee, bottled water, and sandwiches for the group. Luke confirmed that he had two other people coming. With Pastor T's disciples, there would be seven.

Glancing around the café seating area, Pastor T did a second take at a table back in the corner. There was Phil with six other college-age kids. Phil gave T a "thumbs-up" and went right back to the group conversation. Wondering what was going on, T smiled and took the pot of coffee into the private room.

Pastor T's disciple delegation arrived as a group, and shortly after that Luke's invites came. He had invited Leah and a young person by the name of Dex.

Each of them started to take a seat with one delegation on one side of the table from the other delegation. T opened with, "Let's get this off on the right foot. We're not choosing sides like two parties negotiating. Mix it up! I'll sit with my back to the door so you can't get out." Everyone laughed and moved to a different spot around the table. This made for some informal introductions and some immediate conversation. "Luke, can you introduce your friends?"

"Yes, it's my pleasure to introduce—" Luke started with Leah, Dex, and then himself.

Dex was a twenty-two-year-old junior at the college majoring in art education. He had never really gone to church and was taught by his parents that he was his own security. Others could not really be relied upon to help with his future. He and Luke had struck up a friendship. At this point Dex was open to "trying out" Luke's God without any long-term commitment. T introduced Van, Mick, and Dan. He gave a brief explanation of their interest in this meeting. Pastor asked that they start with prayer to our heavenly Father.

Praying for God's guidance was different in this setting. T addressed the diversity within the group and prayed for the Holy Spirit's presence to guide them in a refreshing and innovative solution to carry on God's work and build His kingdom.

"Amen!" Pastor looked up and said, "Maybe I could shed some light on why we're here. I want to reference the Scripture in the Book of Luke *(NKJV)*. First, Jesus calls the disciples to Himself. Keep your attention on 'call.' That's why we are here today. He called each of us to be here at this moment to do something important in His ministry.

"Secondly, after calling His disciples, He designed opportunities to build their faith and ministries. The key word is 'build.' Our job today is to design a method or process where we can intentionally build up awareness and strengthen faith in Christ here in the Village."

Holding up three fingers, T continued, "After the calling and building phases, Jesus sent His disciples to do God's work. Please give your attention to the word 'send.' Jesus turned the ministry over to His disciples. Whatever we come up with today will ultimately send people into life's journey with the tools and confidence to do God's work. We are called, built, and sent." Pausing and looking at Van, T explained, "I've asked Van to kick off the meeting with a few comments."

"Pastor asked me to comment on the send portion. I'll call it 'missional.' Pastor called about fifteen of us together at church to be taught and mentored by him for a two-year period. That's where we are right now—in the build stage. The three of us are here today to hopefully fulfill the send phase or to get outside the walls of the church. We want to involve members of our Disciples Group in a real-world situation where we can create Christian relationships with others who might need a friend." With strong conviction in his voice, Van exclaimed, "Missional is not coming to church to be served but going out to serve!" Glancing over at Luke, he said, "Luke, tell us a little about your expectations."

"Thanks, Van. After thinking about this for a week, I see our being here as a three-legged stool." Luke used his fingers to display his three points. "One leg represents the disciples wanting to be involved in a relational ministry, to be there for the people with whom they can develop Christian relationships. The second leg is a venue where we can involve young people of the Village to gather and share talents and interests. The third leg is the spiritual growth dimension for all of us to grow together."

Luke formed a circle with his hands to symbolize the seat of the stool. "The stool itself represents a multi-dimensional ministry where all parties grow in their respective roles. Some will be mentors or teachers, others will be casual participants, and still others will be searching for in-depth understanding of

Scripture. The combination is off the wall, but there is so much room to grow."

Pastor T was delighted that Van and Luke had taken such leadership roles. "This is really good stuff!" Waving his clipboard, he continued, "I want to throw in what Todd told me in a phone conversation we had this morning."

Pastor T explained Todd's concept of a venue to display and participate in the various arts, the unstructured format, and the intentional availability to grow in faith. T invited everyone to address the group with their ideas. Dex volunteered first.

"I'm coming into this cold," he said as he stroked his beard, "but it's shaping up in my mind to be a show and tell for the arts. Young artists, using that term broadly, can work, display, entertain, and belong without the guidelines of a club membership. I'm not sure I want a steady diet of Jesus, but I understand that getting to know Jesus is the whole purpose."

Leah, tossing her long blond hair, responded, "Since I'm the token woman, I'll give you my opinion. It's like we are all on the same page for our vision, but we're talking like we already have a place to meet. I'd be opposed to meeting in a church. Also, we'd better be realistic about how often we're going to meet and for how long each time."

"Good observations, Leah." Mick felt it was time for Van to talk about his building. "Van, are you willing to share your thoughts about the place you suggested earlier?"

Van nodded, but he felt a need to explain a few things. "First, I think that all of us agree that this gathering place should not be in a church. This needs to be a venue that you and other young people can feel comfortable in and know that there is no motive or deception to get you to join our church. Another thing is you must buy into this as your own ministry. Our role as disciples is to build trust. We want to support and help as partners to create a Christian culture. At the same time, everyone should have fun and find it compelling to come and participate.

"I have a building that's now used for storage. It'll require some clean up, but if we can agree that it'll be used as a Christ-centered ministry, I'll be happy to free up about 25 percent of the space with one stipulation."

Leah wasn't shy about asking. "What's the stipulation? Is it a deal breaker?"

Van made eye contact with those around the table. "We establish a board or council to oversee both the ministry and the building. This group will have to be accountable as good stewards of what happens to the building and what happens in the building. I am asking that this council act in compliance with the purpose we set up for the ministry."

"Cool!" Luke leaned forward and pumped his arm. "I wasn't expecting such a generous gesture—this is like God opening the door of opportunity. Dex, my friend, I really want your input. You represent the young people who might be a little lukewarm to an emphasis on a ministry that focuses on Jesus as our Savior."

"Okay, I'll be as direct as possible. Like many of the young people in the Village, I'm not ready for an 'in-your-face Jesus confrontation.' But I don't think that's what you're talking about. I'd participate if I'm allowed to come as I am with all my doubts and imperfections. You see, I don't want to be embarrassed about my lack of Bible knowledge, nor do I want to be railroaded into a fast track to salvation."

Stroking his beard again, Dex went on, "Just appreciate that I'm not certain where I stand with God, but I am curious. I do like the attraction of mingling with other people who appreciate the value of each other's talents. That's kind of a security blanket for me. I believe at first there'll be some intimidation. I guess it'll be up to all of us to help people feel comfortable."

"Thanks, Dex, for your honesty." Pastor could start to see the pieces, but he felt something was missing. "You are teaching me so much about alternative approaches to ministry." He continued writing down more notes. "Leah, what did you have in mind about the question of being realistic?"

"Well, is this a building that's open just certain hours with a scheduled time for social time, sharing, Biblical presentation, and discussion? I can't pinpoint why I'm uneasy, but it has something to do with getting out of control."

Luke pointed in her direction, saying, "Leah, fortunately your perspective is very focused. I have a thought: imagine a wall of vending machines for snacks and beverages with a disco globe hanging from the ceiling. Just kidding. Really, I believe that we must keep a big vision, but we have to start small, maybe one night a week and use it as a hangout with some intentional sharing and discussion. Leah, how does that sound?"

"Thank you, Luke!" she replied, casting a warm smile of acceptance. "I agree! It might get away from us if we try to do a mega thing. With it open one evening a week for about three hours, we can adjust our approach as we see how people are responding. The real goal seems to be the impact of the one night a week. How do people think, act, and talk when they leave the weekly get-together?"

Dan spoke up, "I haven't spoken yet, but that is really perceptive, Leah. Our Disciples Group could fit into the get-together by one or two of us showing up each week with possibly some refreshments and just trying to get to know the young people who come to participate."

Mick followed with, "Yes, I concur that our role is not to take over but to support and generate relationships. It may not sound like much, but if we, as disciples, come with the right heart and reflect Christian values as we enjoy each other, the relationships may be bigger than we can imagine. My mind is going in the direction of what we as disciples can do with those relationships. Other ministries may spin off of the core venue we're establishing."

Mick's comment about spin-off ministries sounded good to Pastor T. "Frankly, this is new turf for me." Pausing, with a serious look on his face, he ventured, "The formal church is all about organization and structure. Most of what I've done in my ministry is in contrast to what we are talking about. I endorse every inch of what you are saying, and I'm pleased that everyone is talking about relationships and the impact of a life-changing process. My wife, Lil, would be clicking her heels at that endorsement.

"It appears that we agree to minimize formal structure, but Luke talks about being intentional. Let's talk about the difference between formal structure and intentional. Luke, please explain."

Pleased that he could share his wisdom, Luke said, "Being intentional does require some structure. Everyone should have some structure in their life. I guess what I'm talking about is avoiding the idea that every session follows a rigid order. Being brought up as the son of a pastor, I felt I was forced to fit a mold of what church was all about. It started with the invocation, and every Sunday it was the same formality. I have to admit, I started feeling like a robot. That's what I want to avoid."

Leah was jumping at the chance to speak. "Amen, Luke! Can we pray together?" They all looked at T and bowed their heads. "You see, you all did the same thing. You bowed your head and expected the pastor to recite a prayer. Now let's do it differently." Leah asked everyone to stand, clasp the hand of the person next to them, and stand closer together. "Now, I'm going to ask each of you to close your eyes and look upward so you feel God's warmth on your face. Imagine His radiance filling your body with His love. He loves you and me so much.

"I know all of you have something to say to God right now—even if it is only one sentence. Release it from your heart and let God know what is on your mind right now." She squeezed Dex's hand, indicating he should start. "Dex, would you start? And everyone hop in when you are ready."

"God, I have never done this! My words may not be good enough for You, and it might not be what You want to hear, but my heart tells me that You are real. I am not sure what that even means or how I fit in Your world. At this point I have trouble saying, 'thank You' because of all the chaos going on in my heart and mind.

"If You can look beyond that," Dex continued, his voice cracking, "I'm compelled to ask You to help me understand You better and help me come to realize the pleasure of being in Your family as I see it in the eyes and heart of my friends Luke and Leah. Just maybe, God, You're working on me to influence my parents who do not know You at all. If that's the case, You have to help me do this. I don't know how."

Van volunteered, "Lord, heavenly Father, this is such a joy to know that You brought us together this noon. Yes, we're planning a Christian gathering process here in the Village, but You are also using this to help each of us grow to be a little more like Your Son, Jesus.

"I pray You consume Dex's heart and mind with Your promises. I'm honored to be at his side as he spoke what was on his heart. I love You, God. I truly want to serve You by offering what I have to this Village ministry. I ask the presence of Your Holy Spirit to be with all of us and guide us to do what is right in Your eyes."

Everyone took their turn talking to God, their faces turned to the heavens and their grips tightening on the person next to them as the words poured from their hearts. Leah ended the group prayer by saying, "Oh, God, You are awesome. As we have taken turns talking to You, my love for You and my friends in this circle has exploded. There's no end to Your love and mercy. We don't deserve Your kindness. We know there's not enough we can do to pay our debt back to You. Yet, You forgive us. You extend Your unconditional love to us every moment of every day.

"How can we not believe in Jesus and the redemption He made possible for us by dying and then through His resurrection ensuring that we have a life with You forever?

"I pray for my friend Todd and thank You for his recovery. I also pray for the family of the man killed in that accident. Bring them Your peace. Help our decisions to be Your will, and we ask You to bless the results. In Jesus name we pray—Thank You, Jesus! Amen."

There was a moment before everyone released hands when their grips tightened and each person kept their eyes closed as though they had one little message left in their mind to transmit to God. They all sat down, and Pastor T attempted to summarize.

"Thank you, Leah! You have a gift of uniting us in prayer." Looking down at the notes on his clipboard, he continued, "First, I'm so impressed. As Van said earlier, we can all consider that we are sent by God for this Village ministry. We all need to lean on Him for guidance and growth as we refine the—you know, we should consider a name for it. I have heard 'The Gathering,' 'Get-together,' 'Village Venue,' 'Show and Tell,' 'God's Gifts,' and I suppose you have more. Think about a name for next time.

"Before we leave, let's go around the circle to see if there is a commitment to proceed. Let's each of us explain briefly what we see as our role. I'll start. I see my role as working with all of you as a council to expand an understanding of Jesus and how we might build this ministry to mirror what Jesus did with His disciples so it is not just a place to gather but a place to equip people to be sent out to influence others with a Christian relationship and a Christian witness."

"The three of us in the Disciples Group met earlier this week to discuss this," Van explained. "We're in agreement that we support the position you've taken. We'll rotate our people to attend the weekly gatherings and be there demonstrating Godly character but not taking over. We feel we must pray, learn, and grow through these relationships ourselves, and eventually God will use these relationships for something beyond our current comprehension. I see our effort as a never-ending process focused on 'missional' with the involvement constantly reaching out to others with the same message. The Village venue is only the start.

"I'll draft a short version of the council's role relating to my stipulation," Van concluded.

"I came here thinking that I'd just tag along," quipped Dex. "I see now that I can bring people to our gathering who might see things as I do. Starting as a participant and working the crowd with our various artistic abilities might be where I fit.

"For example, I want to bring a couple of my stained-glass projects. I know people will be interested in how it is done and why I like to be creative. Others that I know will bring their paintings, marquetry, paper artistry, pencil drawings, etc. I suppose it can be a show-and-tell format and time for questions. Not everyone has to bring their stuff at the same time. Maybe we could feature an artist each week. I can find the artists."

It was no surprise that Leah was the organizer. "I'm the navigator. I think we all agree that there must be some 'hang out' time for people to just enjoy each other. Then what Dex can drum up in artistic resources, I can bring to life with the 'Feature the Artist' concept and facilitate a discussion about the art itself.

"I won't be able to do that without some spontaneous reference to God being responsible for our passions and expecting us to use them for his glory. No sermons—just expressions of faith. Facilitating comes easy for me, so I feel comfortable getting people engaged in the conversation. Whatever we do, God's love and our love for each other must be contagious."

Leah added, "I feel there should also be an opportunity the last hour or so to break down into conversational groups as we wrap up the evening. I'd like one person, like Pastor T, Luke, or the disciples and even others as we grow, to be designated to explain a Scripture in the Bible and relate it to our lives. That should take about five to seven minutes. We can follow with maybe three to five questions to discuss in our pods. Luke, Todd, and I can facilitate the pod discussions."

Luke responded with, "Amazing! God already knew our gifts. His handiwork is coming to life in this discussion. As far as my role, I'm not the organizer like Leah or resourceful person like

Dex. I function more strategically, constantly following that path to the ultimate destination. I see that as developing a missional culture for everyone who participates.

"Although I need to grow a lot in Biblical knowledge, I feel Todd and I can act in a teaching capacity. I'd like to be an understudy of Pastor T and even join the Disciples Group he has going in his church. I might function pretty well with the help of Dex, Todd, and Leah to create a functioning council. I'm hoping that maybe one disciple and Pastor T will serve in that capacity also."

After an hour of discussion, Pastor concluded, "It's time! We got a lot done in a short time. From my point of view, we just added many pieces to the puzzle. I would suggest we meet at Van's building next week on Wednesday at noon. Maybe we'll have something there to eat. Leah, could you update Todd and invite him to attend? I like the idea of using our Disciple ministry as a primary resource for spiritual growth with the focus on making more disciples with Jesus' at our side."

Luke inquired, "Hey, we must owe you something for the lunch, Pastor." T responded with, "My treat! Is everyone as excited and committed as I am?"

Everyone made an affirmative gesture. Luke with a "thumbs-up," Dex with a pump of the arm, Leah with both hands in the air, and each of the disciples nodding their heads "yes!"

Everyone exchanged a handshake—Leah hugged everyone. They left heading in different directions. T confirmed with the three disciples that they would put something together for the Disciples Group on Monday. T returned to the church, where he was facing a busy afternoon.

Coming on to the church property, he noticed Phil sitting on a bench. Pastor walked over to him and said, "Hey, Phil. What's happening?"

"Hi, Pastor, God is good! He not only gave opportunity for Kyle and me to cement our relationship, He brought several college kids to the forefront of some meaningful spiritual discussions. I know you have tons of things to do. I'll fill you in later." Walking toward the building entrance, T replied, "I'll look forward to that, Phil."

By the time 5:30 p.m. rolled around, T headed for his truck and drove home. Lil had potatoes in the oven. As soon as he entered the door, she gave him a plate with two steaks.

"T, can you start the grill and toss these on? Six minutes on each side." Pastor responded, "Yes, dear. And then I have a lot to tell you."

T loved to grill because he could grab a beverage and sit for a few minutes while the grill did its job. The smell of grilled food made it even more enjoyable. He sat there on the bench alongside the outdoor grill thinking and smiling about the day. The steaks were finished. T brought them in the house, where Lil had everything else ready. He prayed—and then he started talking about his day.

"Lil, remember this morning when I said this was God's day to take us by the hand? Well, He literally led all of us to a common belief of what this Village ministry should be. My story is long, Lil, but tell me first about your day."

LOOKING FOR MEANING:

1. Would you say that being "called" is sometimes a feeling that God places in your heart? Have you ever felt "called"?

2. What did you find unique about the prayers Leah initiated?

3. How did God use each person's gifts to pull the Village project together?

Chapter 9—Surrender!

"May the God of hope fill you with all joy and peace as you trust in him, so that you may overflow with hope by the power of the Holy Spirit."
Romans 15:13 *(NIV)*

God is the source of eternal hope. Hope comes through Scripture and is applied in every believer's heart by the Holy Spirit.

Chapter 9 demonstrates a need to trust each other and God. It is beneficial to find that Christian person you can trust and also place your total trust in God. Your Spiritual growth will be faster and more complete.

Surrender!

Friday was Pastor's usual day to pull together an outline for his Sunday message. Sitting in his office early in the morning, T recalled how the previous Friday he had roughed out the outline for his sermon and JJ had changed all that. With JJ's permission, last Sunday's sermon was titled, "My Friend in Cardboard Boxes." Intrigued and curious best described the worshipers last Sunday. They would be expecting more of the story. This coming Sunday T wanted to add a dimension showing that God is working in JJ's life. T had scribbled a few titles on his notepad, including "Falling Through the Cracks," "Who's Watching Your Back," "From Streets to Safety," and "Where Was God?" He decided to wait until he talked with JJ this noon—if JJ showed up.

Since there had been no word from JJ about their luncheon, Pastor T thought how disappointing it would be if JJ bailed. T had been looking forward to the meeting all week.

With his eyes closed and running his fingers through his wavy black hair, as he did frequently when deep in thought, T allowed the events of the last couple weeks to flash through his mind. For some reason his recollections stopped on Liz and her daughter. Compelled to talk with her to see how things were going, he dialed her work number from the card she had given him after the tour. T received a very professional greeting from a receptionist. After being transferred to Liz's administrative assistant, he was almost certain that Liz would be in some high-level meeting and not available; in fact, he now felt it might be in poor judgment to call her at work. A voice answered and asked how she could help. When T introduced himself, he was interrupted by the administrative assistant.

"I presume you are 'the' Pastor T who Liz talks about? You made quite an impression."

"Well, I'm Pastor T—I hope Liz's comments were good?"

"Oh, they were! I think Liz would like for me to tell you something. She received a call from the school early this morning. All I know so far is that her daughter is the victim of bullying. Liz left immediately, and she hasn't called back yet."

"If I remember right, her daughter's name is Joey. How might I help?"

"Liz is a caring mother, and Joey is her top priority. She has confided in me that the one person she would like to talk with if she ever had to wade through a serious family issue is you."

"Liz so loves that girl." Pastor felt it was a desperate moment for Liz. He replied, "When she calls, give her my cell number, the one I'm calling from now, and ask her to call me."

"I'll tell her, Pastor. Thank you for your concern. Liz and her daughter are like family to me. I'll be praying also."

Pastor sat running his fingers through his hair again, his eyes closed. T said a prayer for Liz and Joey. He kept thinking how devastated Liz must be. This problem was something she could not fix with status, money, or position.

T glanced at his watch. The black onyx dial with a diamond at the twelve o'clock position reminded him of his dad. He slowly removed the watch from his wrist, turned it over, and read the inscription on the back side. It said, "Son, God will not let you down! Love, Dad."

He remembered his dad's eyes watering as he gave the watch to T a few days after Lil was diagnosed with breast cancer. Although it was ten years ago, it was like yesterday. All the doctor consultations, surgery, treatment, and emotional adjustments reminded T how he felt so out of control and then so comforted when he handed it over to God. He knew that Liz would probably have the same feeling. He grabbed a pamphlet titled, "Why, God—Why?" He might just need it if he caught up with Liz sometime today.

Entering the Village, his attention was focused on what the conversation might be with JJ. The Coffee Grounds Café was not too busy, so T took a coffee mug and had it filled as he walked to a table where he and JJ could talk. The minute and hour hands were just passing the diamond on the face of his watch. He thought, "JJ, please show up!" T sat sipping on his coffee for another five minutes, feeling like he had just been stood up, and then his cell phone rang. It was Liz!

With a controlled voice, Liz asked, "Pastor, if you have the time today, I'd like to meet with you about this situation at school. If you don't mind, I'd very much enjoy bringing Joey with me."

Just then, JJ walked in the door of the café and got a big wave from T to come to the table.

"By all means, Liz. I'm so glad you called. I've been praying for the two of you. Right now I'm involved in a meeting away from the church, but I'll be back to the office at 2 p.m.—would that work for you?"

"Yes, that will be perfect. I'm so grateful. Joey and I will see you at two o'clock."

JJ sat down as T finished his conversation with Liz. "You won't have to face this alone—God's blessings." Pastor holstered his phone and turned his attention to JJ.

"Hey, dude—sounds like another hand-holding situation! You make it sound like God solves all the bad things that happen in people's lives."

"And 'hi' to you, too! I was concerned you would not show. What do you say we get something to eat?"

"Dude, you were serious, right? About buying lunch?"

"Of course, JJ—and I'm also serious about hearing your plans for a music repair studio."

"Hey, now it's a studio? I called it a 'man cave.'"

"Whatever! It looks like it's soup and sandwich. Take what you want, JJ."

They both made their lunch selections. JJ chose to order water instead of coffee. T picked up the tab, and they returned to their table. Still needing reassurance, JJ said,

"You know, Pastor Dude, I'm getting the notion you aren't just jerking my leg. Most people don't really mean what they say. Your slugging average is awesome."

"JJ, is that part of the reason you were late?"

"Well, yeah! I was camped out in the park across the street and saw you come into the Village. You see, I haven't figured out your con game yet. Man, it can't be for my money—I ain't got any! That's why I asked if you were buying."

Realizing JJ still felt vulnerable, Pastor said, "I want you to know how much Jesus loves you and what He did to give you a chance to be in His family forever. No game! No scam!"

"There you go again. I'm gett'n used to the words, but I've no idea what you're talking about. Dude, in my world, that's a scam."

"You know what, JJ? I think God's working on your heart. You want to know more, but your street skeptics keep casting doubts—like don't trust anyone."

Pausing to think, JJ replied, "Something like that! You're a dude that came out of nowhere. I get more trusting when we talk, but in between times something says, 'Run!' Catch it, man?"

"Yes, I completely understand. In my world that's the devil talking. He's always working against what God—"

JJ interrupted, "Enough, dude! Now you're talking a gang war between the God Gang and the Devil Dogs—the good and the bad! The only difference between the streets and your world is that they're not real people. In my world, they're both dangerous.

My friend called 'em street bullies. They don't care who they hurt; they just want to control."

"Take my word, JJ, Jesus doesn't want to hurt you—I don't want to hurt you. At some point, you have to trust someone. I hope it's me, but more importantly, God! Let's talk about your music repair dream."

"Before we go there, your phone call sounded next to urgent. Man, if you want trust, let me in on your world."

"Okay! You should relate to this because you mentioned street bullies. Well, we have school bullies also. My friend Liz experienced that with her daughter this morning. Joey, an innocent eight-year-old, was bullied at school. I don't know the details, but I'm meeting with them at two o'clock this afternoon."

"So—what you gonna do? On the streets we either join 'em, run, or fight. We don't have a pastor dude to tell us it's God's plan and we'll be a better person because of it."

"You know more about God than you're letting on. What's your story, JJ?"

"Oh, just another day on the street."

"Tell me! Let your guard down—I promise I'll only tell my congregation."

JJ couldn't help but laugh. "That's your con! How did it go last Sunday?"

"JJ, they're waiting for more. I'd like to tell them that God is working in you."

"Dude, you're a dreamer!"

"I think God is working in you—that's why you're struggling with trust right now. You have a different feeling, and you're not sure how to deal with it. That's why you came today. JJ, tell me the bully story."

With a look of fear in his eyes, JJ began, "Hey, man—you scare me. You always seem to know what is going on inside me. The bully story ain't much. After being on the streets for a few years, the King and I made a bad choice and thought that this one gang would share their shelter with us. They acted as if they welcomed us, but in the middle of the night we were surrounded by about twelve members of the gang. I remember waking up and hearing the jingling of chains and a chant of, 'Kill.' They each had a chain that they used to whip their rival gangs. Mostly they would fling the chains to wrap around your legs or neck to bring you to the ground. From there it was all over. They would either finish beating you with the chains or carve you up with their blades."

"What happened, JJ? Please continue."

"King told me to run. I tried, but two of them swirled their chains and wrapped them around my legs. The thing I remember is the pain as the two chains hit and as I fell like a tree on my face in the rocks of a railroad track. The next thing I felt was a knife across my throat and my long hair knotted up in this guy's fist with a lot of swear words threatening me that my head would be found in the garbage."

"Wow, there's a lot going on here. What happened to your friend?"

"They had already slashed him up, so he was bleeding and left on the ground to bleed out. I knew I was a dead kid—they don't leave witnesses. As the rest of the gang came over to me, they chanted, 'Kill, kill, kill!' The guy with the blade to my throat was supposed to draw it and bleed me out. Man, this was some kind of test of a new gang member. We were on the ground with him on my back. His mouth was right by my ear. He whispered, 'This is your lucky day, kid! Play dead.' He suddenly drew the knife and pushed my face into the stone. I heard someone yell, 'Let's get out of here!'

"After they left, I felt my throat with my hand. There was blood, but the guy just nicked my skin. It was my lucky day."

"JJ, you have me terrified. What did you think at that moment?"

"Man, I felt lucky! But I was concerned about King. As I got up, someone helped me to my feet. I thought they'd come back, so I started swinging. As I turned, I saw it was a guy with a backward collar—a priest. Now you are going to say, 'God sent him!'"

"The thought entered my mind. That's not the end of the story, is it?"

"No! This priest was a big dude. I found out later that he had a boxing gym for kids in the inner city. He had a gang member plant that sent out an SOS when things started going bad that night. That's what saved me.

"The priest gave me a rag and told me to put pressure on my neck. Then we went over to King, who wasn't moving. The priest checked his pulse and said, 'He is still alive. Help me get him in the car.' We drove to the emergency room of the hospital while I sat in the back seat with King.

"He had one bad knife wound on his shoulder. It was bleeding, and the priest keep saying, 'Bro, put your hand on it and keep the blood in.' I freaked out as the blood oozed through my fingers, but I was able to stop most of the bleeding. At the hospital people, in white uniforms rushed King out of sight. The priest stayed with me and had a nurse look at my neck. They put about a dozen stitches in and cleaned me up."

"The priest was your guardian angel, JJ. Did you ever get a chance to talk to him?"

"Yeah! He stayed with me while King was in surgery. Man, I remember someone coming and asking the priest who was going to pay for this. In his deep voice, I can still hear him say, 'Do it out of love, and you'll get repaid! You've got a life to save—that's why God made you doctors and nurses.' They must have heard this before, because they just said, 'Yes, Father!'"

"I can't imagine how scared you were."

"Dude, I was scared for sure, but for some reason, my guardian angel made me feel safe. You know, Pastor Dude, I remember the priest saying, 'Hey kid, life's a battlefield, and you're alive right now because God has a different plan for you. He sees something special in you. Somewhere, sometime, He is going to use you to build His kingdom.' Man, those words still haunt me.

He also said, 'If you spend your life getting even with these kids instead of loving 'em, it will consume you.'"

"What do you think he meant by 'it will consume you'?"

"It flew right over my head at the time, but I think he meant that there's good in everyone in the right situation. Also, I think he was telling me to not carry a grudge but forgive them or I'd be miserable myself.

"The priest dude invited us to stay in a back room of the gym. While King was recuperating, the priest taught me how to box. About the time King was on his feet, I was getting pretty good. I wanted to stay, but King said we couldn't take charity. The priest gave us some advice as we left: 'Man, Satan is your enemy, but Jesus is your Savior—listen to God!'"

"That's good advice, JJ! Why should the priest saying that God has a plan haunt you?"

"Cuz that's not my world! First, I'm not sure I believe it and secondly, I don't know anything about God."

"Don't sell yourself short! You're a smart person who has a great heart. I do believe you want to do this—maybe you're a little frightened about your comfort zone, but that's expected. Let me help!"

"Frightened! Dude, that's an understatement. I do trust you—but those I trusted have disappeared from my life. Man, I don't want to be set up again. It's best we go our own ways."

"That won't happen—and you're stuck with me! Are you ready to talk about your music repair business?"

"Dude, are you kidding? That's all I have been thinking about."

The two of them spent another forty-five minutes identifying what the business should look like, the ideal location, and who might be JJ's customers. Pastor asked if he could say a prayer before they broke up their meeting. JJ reluctantly agreed. JJ was quite shocked when T grabbed his hand and started his prayer.

Before leaving, T asked JJ again about meeting with some people in a small informal gathering. JJ responded, "That scares me more than a knife at my throat, but dude, I trust that you will not put me in a situation I can't handle."

"Great, JJ! God will give you the strength. Can we meet again next Friday? Let's meet in front of the Coffee Grounds. I might want to visit another place." JJ nodded as they butted fists and turned in different directions.

There was plenty of time for T to walk back to the church before the meeting with Liz and Joey. He took his time thanking God for helping him to gain JJ's trust. Pastor T kept thinking about Luke's statements: "You're wasting your time with JJ. He's a loner and a street bum." He then switched to the memory that JJ still carried with him about the priest, "Love 'em or it will consume you." T said to himself, "JJ was able to discern that he had to forgive. God's presence is evident."

T's thoughts went to Joey. What we do and what we say really hurt people. Luke was a good Christian and probably didn't mean what he said, but when people are different from us, we like to portray them as though there's something wrong with them. T impulsively said, "That's wrong!" A little embarrassed, he looked around to see if anyone heard him.

Before entering the church, he stopped and watched the little kids from the day care playing in the playground. They were so happy and innocent, trusting that nothing would ever happen to them that would make their lives difficult. It was sad, but also he realized joy that God, through His Spirit, would help them and give them opportunities to make them spiritually strong.

From his office where he was reading his Bible, he heard the patter of feet running down the hall. A young blond girl with a wonderful smile stopped at his open door.

Standing and walking over to her, he said, "You must be Joey?"

"How did you know? Who told you my name?"

Kneeling down in front of her, Pastor said, "Your mommy told me you were coming."

Looking up at her mother, she asked, "Did you, Mom?"

"Yes, I did, honey." Liz lowered herself closer to Joey. "Pastor T is a friend of mine, and I asked him if we could talk today."

"Mister, can I go out and play with the kids on the playground?"

"If it's okay with your mother, I'll take you out there." Liz nodded permission. "You see, Joey," T said, taking the little girl by the hand, "I have to walk you through the day care building to get to the playground. The kids will only be out there for another ten minutes. Is that okay with you?"

Joey looked up at the pastor. "What do I do then?"

"I can have someone bring you back, or you can do what the kids are doing in their classroom."

"Bye, Joey. You'll be safe out there," reassured her mother.

T returned to his office from the playground area, telling Liz that Joey was a sweet little girl and that she didn't seem to be bothered by the bullying incident.

"I know!" Liz responded, "She keeps telling me that they didn't mean to do it. But from what I understand, this is commonplace with about six girls in the class ahead of Joey. The school officials were very nice, and they know who did the bullying. At this point, they have the police liaison involved and have arranged a meeting with the parents."

"What exactly happened, Liz?"

"Well, in Joey's case, they pushed her down on the grass outside the school several times when she was waiting for her ride. The girls ripped her dress and called her some pretty vulgar names. I guess the name calling has been going on for several weeks. One name that apparently has spread through the school is 'Fart Face' and another is 'Raunchy Rich Bitch.'"

"That is troubling! Why do you think Joey's so calm about it?"

"Her teachers told me that Joey's always so serious about her schoolwork that she doesn't take time to play with the kids. They indicated she has an obsession to get all her work done and is somewhat of a perfectionist. Yet she displays a social behavior of wanting to be accepted by the other kids."

"Liz, are you saying that she is willing to get pushed around and made fun of in order to be accepted by the kids?"

"I hope not, but that's the way it appears. Pastor T, have I gone overboard with the nanny and the private transportation? I suppose Joey wanting to be perfect is my fault, too."

"You don't know that, Liz. But it's a good time to assess how she is responding to all this special attention. It does sound like she is starved for friends. That doesn't excuse the behavior of the bullies. I think the schools have adopted a zero-tolerance policy for bullying. Hopefully, that part of it will be addressed."

"I thought I was the superwoman who could be the perfect parent and a career woman as well."

"Parenting is not a science, Liz! Raising kids is not easy regardless of what you do. You thought you were doing the right thing. Do you and Joey have good talks?"

"Yes, we do. She is pretty open to me and has, in the past, expressed her feelings with no problem."

"Keep that up, Liz! And make sure she knows you love her. Find out how she feels about having friends. See if she opens up about what things she would like to see in her friends. I'm guessing she's quite confused about that and hasn't given it much thought. She's getting to the age where she has to think through her decisions."

"Do you think I should back off on the nanny providing her transportation to and from school?"

"It wouldn't hurt to try it in small doses, but monitor what's going on. I take it she has led a pretty sheltered life. She'll see and hear things that'll shock you. I wish she were in our

Sunday school. Even though it's only once a week, it would expose her to a life with Jesus and some excellent mentors."

"Pastor, I'm willing to do anything. We've been reading Bible stories from a book I had when I was a kid."

"Excellent! Liz, I hope to see you in church on Sunday, too. You might be surprised at my message—I just found a title from my friend, JJ. It will be called, 'Life Is a Battlefield!' It's about bullying—a very deadly, senseless act of violence and what one person, a priest, is doing about it. Out of love, the bullied and the bully are given hope of a new life. Satan's our real enemy. When we listen to God's Spirit, Satan has no control because God is triumphant over the devil."

"Sounds like you have had some experience with bullies, Pastor."

"Not so much, but whatever the struggle in life is, God manages to make us stronger. In some cases, we learn a great deal about ourselves and along the way pick up bits of wisdom. I pulled this pamphlet entitled, *Why God, Why?* You might find it comforting."

Joey came running into the office and hugged her mom. "Hi! The teacher walked me back. That was fun—Mommy, can we do this again?"

"How about Sunday, sweetheart? We'll come to Sunday school and learn more about the Bible stories we've been reading."

Joey looked at Pastor T, saying "Good! Pastor, will you be here on Sunday, too?"

"Yes, I will, Joey. I can't wait to see you and your mom. Joey, can I say a short prayer with all of us holding hands?"

"Cool!" Joey grabbed her mother's hand and extended the other to Pastor T.

"You know what, God? I have a little girl and her mommy here. They're really special people, and they want to know more about You. Please be in their hearts and help them as they make decisions. These are Your children, God, and I know You love them.

Help us all do what is right in Your eyes. In Jesus' name we pray. Amen."

As they walked out of Pastor's office, T heard Joey ask her mother, "What did the pastor mean that we are God's children?"

"Well, Joey, we believe that God's like a father to us. We can't see Him, but He is all around us. You know that He made everything—like the trees, the sky..."

T stood smiling as Liz left the building fielding Joey's questions. As Pastor walked by Jon's office, he poked his head in, saying, "A penny for your thoughts." Jon looked up.

"You caught me studying the four Gospels. I decided to re-evaluate everything Jesus did leading up to His crucifixion and resurrection. I find value in trying to understand Jesus and how I should live a more missional lifestyle."

"Jon, you picked the right book! Thanks for getting on the missional wagon." Pastor reached in his pocket and tossed a penny to Jon. "God bless you, Jon."

That evening, T had a lot to tell Lil. In the conversation, Lil suggested inviting Liz—and possibly others that might be struggling—to their house. T said, "Thought you would never ask. I think JJ finally consented to meet with some people. He has a great story that I think will make a difference."

"By the way, T, I'll pack a picnic lunch for you and JJ next Friday. It sounds like you'll not be at the café. Besides, I wonder if he has ever experienced a picnic with a friend."

"Hey, Lil: why don't you come along? I think JJ would like to meet you. We can sit in the park and have our picnic."

LOOKING FOR MEANING:

1. Have you ever been in a situation like Pastor T when he turned it all over to God when his wife had cancer? How did you feel?

2. On a scale of 1 to 10, where do you feel JJ is right now in placing his trust in Pastor T? Why?

3. On a scale of 1 to 10, where do you feel JJ is right in now placing his trust in God? Why? What is the relationship between question #2 and question #3?

Chapter 10—Go!

"Go therefore and make disciples of all the nations, baptizing them in the name of the Father and of the Son and of the Holy Spirit..."
Matthew 28:19 *(NKJV)*

On the basis of God's authority, the disciples were sent to make disciples of all nations. As followers of Jesus, we are also his disciples with instructions to do the same.

Chapter 10 shows a strong affirmation by the pastor that today's church should be structured to equip the saints inside the church—the disciples—for the purpose of making disciples outside the church.

Go!

On Sunday Pastor T delivered his "Life Is a Battlefield!" message. His congregation was attentive as they absorbed the vivid description of JJ's life-threatening story of the streets.

T engaged the congregation in the thought that bullying at school or on the Internet is just as damaging to a young person as was JJ's experience. Satan, however, is the most dangerous bully of all—constantly working to destroy our faith in God. T challenged the congregation to love and forgive those who try to harm us but not to condone their behavior. Love others and act as God's ambassadors this week and every week to help people who are in need of Jesus. In short, be missional!

"As we go, let's be a true reflection of Jesus. Some of us need to find out more about Jesus in order to do this." Pastor reminded his congregation. "Don't put it off!" he advised. "In addition to attending worship each Sunday, reserve twenty minutes every day to read the Bible and meditate on its meaning. Also, get engaged in a small group and begin sharing with other people how God is working in your lives."

Pastor T was able to spend a little time with Liz between services. Joey skipped up to the two of them, hugged her mom, and said, "I have a new friend! Her name is Dory, and we are going to sit together next Sunday."

Placing his hand on Joey's head, T said, "That's great, Joey! Did you learn about Jesus riding on a donkey?"

"Yes! That guy in the tree really wanted to see Jesus. I know how he feels because I am short and sometimes I can't see what's going on."

Pastor asked Joey, "Why did this guy want to see Jesus?"

"Well, he was kind of a bad guy who stole money from people, but he decided that Jesus was more important. He promised to give all the money back."

"Very good! His name was Zacheus, and he realized that Jesus was sent by God to change his ways and help him get to heaven. Jesus shows us that we must love even those who are hard to love."

Liz responded, "Sweetheart, I'm so glad you liked Sunday school." Turning to T, she said, "I can't thank you enough, Pastor. Joey and I are still dealing with the bullying thing, but we're spending some quality time together. We started inviting friends over to play after school once a week, and I'm not depending on the nanny to do what I should have done in the first place."

"Call me if you want to talk. Say, Liz, would you consider getting together with some other people to just hang out for one evening? The person I talked about in the message today, JJ, is also considering attending."

"Is that a good idea, Pastor? Isn't JJ kind of from the other side of the tracks? He isn't exactly like us!"

"Liz, what would Jesus do? Would he love him?"

Realizing it was the wrong thing to say, Liz replied, "Oh, I'm sorry! I've lived in my ivory tower too long. Please be patient with me. Of course I'd like to get together with other people."

"You should be asking God to give you patience and wisdom. I'm just His tool to carry out His will—and remember, you are, too!"

"I've so much to learn. Joey and I are discussing the Bible each evening before bedtime. I'll probably learn more than Joey. Talk to you again, Pastor!"

T waved good-bye and hurried off to the next worship service. That afternoon, he had a meeting with his Board of Elders at which he felt compelled to introduce a missional process for the church. Pastor started the meeting.

"Welcome, everyone. We should invite God to be part of our meeting. Would you join me in prayer?"

Pastor acknowledged God's power and grace and confessed that we all fall short of His expectations. He thanked God for His patience and guidance. Then T walked around the table touching every man in attendance, calling them by name as he requested the Holy Spirit to be in each heart and mind as they considered a missional emphasis in the church. "In Jesus' name we pray. Amen!"

Cole, the Elders' chairperson, thanked Pastor and reviewed the two items of business: "Pathway to Our Destination" and "The Village Project." He turned it over to Pastor T to explain the significance of the Pathway item.

"Thanks, Cole! I believe our congregation is ready to be challenged for the ultimate service to God and each other. Let's address the item, 'Pathway to Our Destination.' We never really get to the bottom line about our Biblical destination as a church. Tell me: what should be our destination or the ultimate mission of the church?"

Cole felt he knew what Pastor was asking. "I think you're referencing the Great Commission. Jesus makes it quite clear when He gave the command to His disciples—we are to MAKE DISCIPLES!"

"Correct, Cole! As your Pastor, I find it interesting that you use the word, 'command'—and you're right again! Jesus wasn't suggesting. It was a command to His disciples and to us. As the spiritual leaders of His church, we probably will all agree that our Biblical mission is to make disciples. The real debate is what does it mean to make disciples and to what degree are we committed to follow Jesus' command?"

Jake, the Elder the others called "Doubting Thomas" or "DT," added, "It probably goes back to the definition of 'disciple'—which I understand to be 'a follower of Christ.' We're to prepare ourselves and our members to think, talk, and act like Jesus. I believe our congregation feels we're doing a pretty good job of that. The issue, as I understand it, is to be more intentional about taking our congregation to the next level of living out our faith beyond the church walls to make more disciples.

"Pastor, in past meetings, you've referred to this in one word, 'missional.' Today, we are at the crossroad of how we should implement a missional culture in our church. There isn't a person in attendance today who doesn't feel compelled to be more missional, but how we do this is a sensitive debate within the membership of our church. It's misunderstood and overwhelming to most of our members."

"Thank you, Jake—you framed the issue beautifully. This is where the rubber hits the road. A missional effort will take our congregation from being served to a mentality of serving. Jesus said 'Go!' That means that wherever we are or whatever we are doing, we must be prepared to express our faith about Jesus being our Savior. And you're right! It's difficult and overwhelming to a lot of people.

"Acts 1:8a says, 'But you shall receive power when the Holy Spirit has come upon you...' *(NKJV)*. As we have been taught, this means that the Holy Spirit will guide and strengthen us as we engage ourselves in our community creating Christian relationships, in our state and nation, and eventually the world. This brings us right back to your statement relating to 'how intentionally we are leading the congregation to do it.'"

Every board has an "Abe," someone who likes his comfort zone and views challenges from inside his box. Abe spoke up. "Your missional vision suggests that every Christian is capable of being evangelistic. That's hard for me. Not all of us are evangelists."

"You're correct, Abe—at least in the sense that God didn't give everyone the gift of a TV evangelist. But is there any reason why any one of us can't create relationships beyond the church while displaying Christian behavior?"

"Yes, I guess we can," responded Abe reluctantly, "but why do we have to do it outside the church?"

Pastor lowered his voice to almost a whisper. "Because that's where the opportunity exists." Raising his voice to a normal tone, he continued, "Granted, we have people sitting in the pews of our church who require more understanding of Jesus. That's an issue of making disciples internally—growing in Christ. We must create a process for them to grow to the point where they can go outside the church and tell of Jesus and the Good News. We've always placed our emphasis on equipping the saints or making disciples *in* the church, but we forget about why we are doing that. It's to make disciples *outside* the church."

Still not seeing the total picture, Sam asked, "Why can't the Evangelism Committee do it?"

Pastor T seized the opportunity to place responsibility where it belonged. "Because Jesus says it's every Christian's responsibility. That means it's your job and my job as followers of Christ. Remember, our job is to introduce Jesus and help a nonbeliever understand what Christ did for us. It's not to make that person a believer—God will do that!"

"I'm really uncomfortable," admitted Abe. "How do we tell them about Jesus?"

Pastor decided to relate the question to Abe's work life. "Abe, if someone in the parking lot at work were to ask you why you are such a forgiving person, what would you tell him?"

"I guess I'd say that Jesus is my Savior and He forgives my sins. He cared so much that He died on the cross for me and you. I feel I should follow His example of forgiveness."

"Was that so tough? What you just said is a perfect response, and it's missional. In other words, it complies with the Great Commission in Matthew 28."

"I'm not convinced!" stated Jake. "And I'm not ready for this!"

"It's possible that we're not ready," said Bill, the thinker and problem solver of the Elders, "but we're talking about preparing ourselves and our congregation to be missional. I've heard that our ultimate service destination is to follow the Great Commission—making disciples! We prepare ourselves inside the church, and we execute by creating Christian relationships with people who don't know and understand Christ. Our mission opportunity is outside the church living our Christian faith to influence others wherever life takes us. I'm comfortable with that, but now we must identify the process to do this and finally communicate it effectively to our membership. Pastor, I think I'm ready for your 'Pathway.'"

"Thank you, Bill. So let's get to the pathway I'm talking about. Better yet, let's call it a process that's intentional about leading our congregation to that destination."

Sam interjected with his perspective. "I'm not sure our congregation is ready for this, but as a businessperson I can relate to your thinking. There isn't a successful organization or business that doesn't strategically and intentionally create the process to achieve their vision."

"The body of Christ is not a business, but that doesn't excuse us from being intentional about our strategy to be effective," Pastor T agreed. "I have a book I want all of you to read. It's called *Simple Church*,[4]" he said as he passed the books to everyone in attendance.

As Abe thumbed through the book, he mentioned what most people would not bring up. "Pastor, I'm a little surprised that you are advocating a systematic approach. I've always had the impression that pastors would prefer to avoid accountability and wait for the Lord to provide."

"Good point! I'm on both sides of that scenario. We do have to be patient for God's timing and open to where He wants us to go. But God can't act until we begin the process of moving people to be more missional. As far as pastors are concerned, we've never been taught how to play a strategic role in the church.

"If we listen to Scripture carefully, the Holy Spirit gave each of us at least one gift and told us to use it for God's glory. It would be irresponsible to not use the gifts of administration, leadership, teaching, serving, discernment, faith, giving, etc. to improve effectiveness and accountability in His church."

Wanting to move things along, Jake said, "That makes sense. Personally I like your logic, Pastor, but I'm hesitant to make a commitment until the congregation has been more involved. But please proceed with the staff's perception of being more intentional."

"The process has to be simple, and it must be Biblical. *Simple Church*[3] mentions several churches that have developed a process of simplicity that keeps them on track for missional service. We don't want to copy them, but we can learn from them. These churches have carefully chosen two or three statements that they feel are the most compelling Biblical characteristics to move their congregations to make disciples. For example, 'Love' is one common Biblical value and one of Jesus' commands." Pausing, T looked directly at Bill. "Bill, it looked like a light bulb went on. Do you want to say something?"

"Are you saying that we should analyze our ministries, our staffing, and our volunteerism and then decide how they support loving God and each other? If they do, we know that the ministry is contributing and moving people on the pathway to what we want to become—missional. If the ministry doesn't fit, it's using energy and money that isn't contributing to our destination?"

"Bill's analogy is great," Cole emphasized. "I can see that all staff and ministries would establish their goals around these two or three statements. This, by itself, would give the church focus and energy to all move in one direction. Obviously there are some management mechanics to work out. Pastor, can you be more specific?"

"I'm trying to introduce the book *Simple Church* as an example. As a staff, we have another set of statements that might fit our church a little better. Some of you are familiar with establishing core values for an organization. In all cases, the core values represent what will contribute the most to the vision. In other words, if the core values are taken seriously and implemented effectively, the result will be faster and more favorable progress in achieving the mission or vision.

"Some organizations use core values to hang on the wall as a promise to their customers. Others structure their entire management process around making incremental improvement toward these values, knowing that core value effectiveness is the pathway to achieving their ultimate destination. As a staff, we're suggesting the latter because it creates credibility, accountability, and manageability.

"The staff has endorsed three values that we feel will serve as the process to guide our leadership, staff, and ministries to be more missional. You can see them on the screen."

-Energized Spiritual Growth
-Ignited Relationships
-Selfless Serving

Pastor T explained each of the three values and indicated that by establishing a focus on them, members of the congregation would automatically be driven to what they want to become.

Bill spoke up in support of the staff concept. "From a management point of view, I can see two things happening:

"First, the three values become the heartbeat of the organization because they represent the three most significant influencers to create a missional culture. They automatically imply movement because of their diversity.

"Second, goals can be directed at one or a combination of the values in a measurable, time-bound, and quantifiable manner, providing the things Pastor has already mentioned—credibility, accountability, and manageability."

Sensing acceptance from the majority, Pastor made one more point. "Bill, your comment about movement is a good observation. We often find people stuck in the Growth mode, for example, because they are comfortable absorbing God's Word. But there's a point where people must move on and share their understanding and eventually become a serving Christian both inside and outside the church."

"Oh, I get it!" Everyone laughed as Sam saw the total picture. "As we develop a mind of Christ, we will want to live it at work, in our neighborhood, socially, etc. Life takes us to many places where we can influence people through our actions, relationships, and words."

Cole tapped on the table to get the group's attention. "Pastor, you have been beating this drum for many months. Personally, I feel there's a lot of potential with your strategic approach. I sense that the rest of the board is warming up to the idea also. However, someone mentioned earlier that it might be advisable to move slowly on this so we can engage the congregation." The heads of other board members were nodding. "Pastor, are you comfortable with this approach?"

"Yes, I am. I realize that this is a big challenge to you and the congregation, but I'm thrilled that you are at least open to the idea of a more missional culture. Cole, your thoughts are excellent. Let's use the next few weeks to listen to God and see where He seems to be taking us. At our next meeting we can discuss a process for implementation. Part of that implementation must include an informational plan for the congregation.

"The second part of our topic today is an update from our Disciples Group. We have present three people who are members of our two-year leadership building process. As you know, we call it the Disciples Group. They've been working on a missional opportunity. I'd like to have them explain the Village project to you."

Cole raised his hand, again wanting the floor. "Before we move to the Disciples Group presentation, I'd like to say that I've been impressed and encouraged about the seeds Pastor T planted this afternoon. We need more focus and clarity if we're going to be effective. We can't let this die. In the framework of commitment from this group, will someone present a motion that we continue our missional dialogue, develop our strategies to become missional, and ask God to be part of our decisions?"

Members of the board quickly responded with a motion, second, and a majority vote to move the missional process forward. One person voted "no" because he thought it was too soon and too complicated.

Cole said, "I'm sorry I interrupted you, Pastor T. Recording our actions in the minutes are important if we're going to declare our leadership to be missional. Please continue."

"That's quite all right! I'm so grateful for your leadership instincts. Now, about the Village project. Van, will you start with what has been done and how you see the Village project becoming a missional opportunity for our church members?"

"Thanks, Pastor. I'd also like to introduce Dan and Mick. All three of us have been involved and will have something to say about the developing opportunity in the Village. Let's start at the beginning when we met with Pastor T."

Van and the other two men reviewed the progress, including the critical meeting with some of the Village young people. Each demonstrated excitement about the upcoming meeting and the possibility of launching the Village concept. Pastor T remained quiet and showed pleasure over the enthusiasm and optimism of the entire group.

At the end, Van fielded some questions. The board chair again said,

"I can't remember a meeting where I've been so encouraged by our role as Christian leaders. Who'll introduce a motion to support the action that's taking place with the Village project?" A motion was introduced and passed to encourage the

Disciples to continue working with the youth in the Village and return to the Board of Elders with final recommendations.

Pastor went to the front of the room. "Thank you, gentlemen. You are aware that this leadership group moved into an action mode today and there will be barriers along the way. The truth is that without commitment to action, God's intervention is limited. The Holy Spirit was here in each of you today, and He will stay with each of you to carry out His will. At the next meeting we'll continue our missional discussion. Let's close in prayer."

Returning to his office, Pastor T checked his emails. There was one from Oz commenting on the JJ message today. He and Ags were touched and felt compelled to ask if they could help in some way. Both Oz and Ags grew up poor and experienced the struggle of escaping some really bad neighborhood situations. They knew how hard it was to bridge the gap between being down and out and being a contributing citizen.

T quickly replied, asking if they'd like to meet JJ—possibly in a small-group setting. He explained that the best thing they could do was to show JJ that there were people in the church who cared about him.

Lil and T sat on the patio relaxing that evening enjoying the serenity of God's work. As a pastor, T knew there were not too many people who could share the best and the worst of one's life. Lil was his best friend, and T treasured the moments when he was surrounded by God's love and Lil's love and understanding. Lil asked T to describe his day in one word.

"Superfragilisticexpealidocious!" he laughed.

"Come on, be serious, T!"

Well, Lil, how about 'frightening'?"

"That's not like you. What do you mean?"

"You know, Lil, we've taken many leaps of faith together, but this is like jumping off a cliff at night, not knowing if I need a parachute or a swimsuit. I've never stretched my leadership this far. Frankly, I don't even know if I'm a leader or if I should be demonstrating leadership. My training was all about Biblical knowledge, doctrine, original script interpretation, and some spiritual counseling.

"Most of us never were taught how to lead. Up until now, I really haven't led. That's confusing to me because Jesus led, Nehemiah led, Moses led. So is it God saying, 'It's time to lead!' or has my ministry just evolved naturally from teaching to leading?"

"Well," Lil replied, "God worked on Moses eighty years before he called him to lead. I'm glad He didn't wait that long to give you the nudge. I've always thought of you as a leader. Like most pastors, you got stuck in the politics and maintenance of the church until now.

"Thank God," she continued. "I feel like a new bride being carried over the threshold. It's so refreshing because you're excited and hopeful again. I also like that you're sharing the ups and downs of this journey. I want to stay on board!"

Leaning over and kissing Lil, T whispered "I love you. Thanks for your support!"

Pastor had a busy couple of days at the church. He sent out email reminders of the meeting at the Village on Wednesday and hoped that JJ would remember their meeting on Friday. Liz called and thanked T for the special attention he gave Joey and her. She indicated that Joey was starting to talk more about the bullying incident at school. It had gone from Joey thinking she had done something wrong to Joey asking, "Why would they do that?" Liz was picking Joey up at school each day, and Joey was responding well to her mother being more available.

Word got out about the Elders' meeting and the discussion on accountability. The first members from whom T received complaints were the turf and silo folks. The "turf folks" are those who are protective of their ministry independence and authority. "Silo folks" refer to those who isolate themselves and their ministries, rejecting collaboration with other ministries. As expected, most of their information was not complete.

Pastor T suddenly became aware that there was no honeymoon when it came to change. He also knew now leadership was lonely but good leaders had to resist the pressure of conceding to the status quo. He knew, too, that he would have to work extra hard to keep the fires from flaring up.

Wednesday came, and T put a few things together for the Village young people's meeting. The entire group had decided to meet at Van's building. T was wondering about lunch, but he decided that the group didn't have to eat every time they met.

T was a few minutes early, and as he walked toward the empty building he saw something taped on the front windows. As he got closer, he read the signs, which said, "Future Home of Village *As We Go Ministries!*" Inside, Van was busy setting up a table of make-your-own sub sandwiches.

"Hi, Van. I didn't know you were going to feed us, too. How can I help?"

"Oh, I came down to clean up the place a little and decided to pick up a few things. If you're willing, you could unpack some of those soft drinks and place them on the table."

Pastor got to work, saying, "Hey, you guys did a good job with the Village project presentation on Sunday at the Board of Elders meeting."

"Thank you," Van acknowledged. "Pastor, I wanted to talk to you about all this organization. Please don't take me wrong. I'm the first one to feel organization at church and in the Village is necessary, but we can't lose sight of why we're doing this. The vision or mission must be our focus. The lost souls we're trying to impact don't care one bit about organization. For example, this building will house a great party; however, it's the relationship and Holy Spirit's influence that's the main thing."

"Wow, and you don't feel you can communicate effectively? I agree 100 percent. It's like Steven Covey's quote, 'The main thing is to keep the main thing the main thing.'"[5]

"I love it! Hey, here they come—all at once." The door opened and four young people entered, looking up, down, and side to side. "Welcome! Come on in and look around. We'll be ready with the sandwiches in a few minutes."

Pastor addressed everyone after Van made all the finishing touches on the table arrangement. "Again, welcome everyone. Please welcome Todd to our group." Everyone clapped; Leah winked and smiled at Todd. "As you know Todd's still recovering from his automobile accident. Glad to see you up and around, Todd. Let's thank God for the things He is doing in our lives."

After T was finished praying, he extended an invitation. "Please grab some food that Van has prepared. Maybe we can sit on the floor by the front window and talk while we eat."

Luke held up his hands to get everyone's attention. "Before we start, I want to express our appreciation to Van for being such a good host. Also, this building is really awesome! Leah, Dex, Todd, and I walked past it yesterday and looked through the windows. We can't believe this! It's like a dream and the alarm hasn't gone off yet." The young people clapped and gathered around Van with handshakes and pats on the back.

"Please help yourself. If I've forgotten anything, let me know."

All eight members dished up some food and sat on the floor or on the front window ledge of the room that measured about sixty by thirty feet. Pastor still had his clipboard. "I jotted down three things that I feel should be decided today. If we get agreement, we should be ready to go!

First is the written building agreement; second, creation of the governing council; and finally, operational planning and launch date.

"Van, would you start by reviewing the draft of the building agreement?"

"Yes. I had an agreement put together making our church the sponsor of the project but the Village Council is the governing body for planning and programming. I will donate the use of the building to the church which in return is obligated by the agreement to make it available exclusively to action by the Village Council in compliance with our missional vision. The agreement must be renewed each calendar year and adopted by mutual consent."

Luke spoke up, "I think we're okay with that!" The young people nodded. "Who'll be on the council? And what's the council's authority?"

Dan stood up with a pile of papers in his hand. "We also drafted a memorandum of understanding that spells out the authority and responsibility of the council. Here, I'll pass it around while Mick gives you the specifics."

"I'll sure try. The memo requires three young people from the Village and two members from our Disciples Group to serve on the council. T feels he should only be involved as a spiritual resource."

Leah had both hands in the air. "You guys are really on it! I like the loose ends tied up in writing."

"Van, has the concept been given a name?" Todd asked. "I see there is reference to *As We Go Ministries*."

"I had that put in because it is a missional process of spreading the Good News of Christ *as we go* in life. It's not carved in stone. If the four of you young folks can brainstorm something better, go for it!"

"I like it!" replied Todd. "I'm proud to be part of something that will touch lives with Jesus. Pastor, is this meant to be the final draft?"

"As I understand, the formal written documents will be reviewed individually by all in attendance today. You should get your suggestions back to Van within a week. He will create a final draft, and we'll meet to finalize organizational documents."

Dex, who didn't care about the legal ramifications, offered, "I guess that brings us to the planning and programming. We did kick that around last time. Does the council do that?"

Luke, seeking direction, said, "Since we don't have a legal *As We Go* council yet, is it okay to get our heads together today and assign each of us a role to play in the programming? From that we can spell out the responsibilities."

"Sounds good to me, Luke," replied Pastor, looking at his watch. "I have another appointment, so I must get moving. Could you be ready to open in two weeks? Or is that pushing it?"

"No! No! We can do it!" responded Leah. "Todd and I will do the decorating and get the signs ready."

"Before I leave, let's ask God to bless this ministry. Todd, would you pray?" Todd asked everyone to form a circle and join hands. He then asked them to talk to God about what was on their heart. He wrapped it up with a challenge to everyone to honor God. As T left, he told Van to let him know what time and what he had to do.

"Part of our function is to keep minutes. Pastor, I'll get you a copy. Today we can formalize the council and get *As We Go Ministries* launched. Turning to the group, he said, "Let's talk first about publicity."

T had a busy afternoon. That evening Lil asked T to heat up the grill for hamburgers.

"My pleasure!" T grabbed a beverage and went out on the patio. After getting the grill started, he dropped into a lounge chair. Running his fingers through his hair with a deep exhale, he looked up and saw a few clouds in the sky moving and making different configurations. He had a moment to reflect on God's awesome creation.

Coming out onto the patio with the hamburger, Lil commented, "You look like you're a hundred miles away."

"I am! More than a hundred! Lil, I don't know what I would do without God's enormous love. I wish everyone would have an open heart to experience His generosity and love. He brought you and me together, and I'm so grateful every time I see what He has given us.

"It makes me feel like I can't let Him down. Van has used the term, *As We Go Ministries* a couple of times and today suggested it as the name for the Village project. I can't get that term out of my head. It is missional! I am so thankful to God that the Holy Spirit is consuming Van's heart. He's a great leader, carrying God's ministry in the right direction."

LOOKING FOR MEANING:

1. How do you relate to the description of missional at the Board of Elders meeting? What is your reaction to the core values staff suggested?

2. We have been taught to "Go, make disciples!" Does the interpretation, "As we go" or "While we are going" make it easier to understand? Why?

3. Did you see the meeting at Van's building as "missional"? In what ways?

Chapter 11—Trust!

> *"Again…Even I live by placing my trust in God. And yet again, I'm here with the children God gave me."*
> Hebrews 2:13 *(Message)*

Jesus, by assuming a human form, shows his reliance on God during his earthly journey.

Chapter 11 demonstrates that trust is the key to any relationship. As we gain someone's confidence, it is easier to talk about Jesus. We also must place our trust in God to help us do His work.

Trust!

As We Go Ministries in the Village was in good hands. The council was organized with Luke acting as the chairperson, Todd as vice chair, and Leah as secretary. They already had publicity in all the prominent spots in the Village. An artist friend of Dex was painting the sign on the window of the building that day.

The council had lined up chairs and tables from a restaurant that went out of business. Leah had arranged daily coverage on the college radio station, and it was possible they would get city-wide publicity on local TV and in the newspaper. They even had an electric coffee maker donated by somebody in the Village network. A bakery was donating rolls and pastries for the first two months.

Van had asked T to be in attendance at the launch to cast the vision to those who attended and also to explain what was meant by, "As we go." Dex was going to display his stained-glass projects and give a short demonstration. He also had lined up a water color artist for the following week. In fact, they had artists lined up for the entire month, and it was part of their publicity.

It was already Friday, and T would be meeting JJ and Lil in the Village for a picnic lunch. T had an idea to get JJ engaged with other people, but he didn't want to scare him off, either.

Pastor, taking the last bite of Lil's delicious bacon, said, "Lil, I hope JJ responds favorably to our good intentions today."

Displaying a puzzled look, Lil said, "Why wouldn't he?"

"We have to be sensitive to JJ's experience on the streets. It wasn't that long ago that he didn't trust anyone and he lived from day to day on his own independence."

"Oh, come on, T! No one is that calloused."

"I can assure you, Lil, JJ has very little reason to trust people. He may even see you as a threat, but it is time he has a few more reliable people in his life."

"Well, I'll try not to act like I'm there to set the hook."

"Those are words that JJ will probably use," T laughed. "How will you react?"

Laughing even harder, Lil said, "Oh, I'll tell him I brought my own landing net."

As he walked toward the door, T advised, "Lil, park the Silver Streak just south of the Village, and I'll meet you there and help carry the picnic lunch. See you then!"

T arrived at the church parking lot in his pick-up. As he walked into the church, T speed-dialed Van on his cell. Van answered.

"Good morning, Pastor!"

"Good morning, Van. I received your email update on the Village project. It sounds like you had a good planning session."

"We had a blast—everything just fell into place," Van agreed. "It was like God handpicked this group. Everyone had something to offer. I hope God blesses us with good attendance. Another thing: we are different ages, and it didn't even matter."

"That's something worthwhile to pray for! Van, I just keep thinking about your concern a few weeks ago that you may not be a good disciple. How do you feel about that now?"

"My feeling the last few weeks is that God has changed me. But that's not true. He's just bringing out what and who I am, and so far it's a good fit. I can't remember a time I felt so fulfilled. Your confidence in me also really means a lot. I'm not really leading— just making sure the pieces get put together."

Opening the door to his office, T said, "Please, take it from me, Van—that's leading! You're very strategic, and you've navigated this boat so it's right on course. We have to remember that God is ultimately in charge. All of us must continually search for understanding in God's Word so we don't lose track of our purpose in the Village."

"Pastor, would you get something in the church bulletin about our missional effort in the Village? I'll email all the men in the Disciples Group. They've been getting bits and pieces at our weekly meetings, but we should celebrate the launching of *As We Go Ministries* in the Village."

"Yes, it's time we bring everyone together on this. I'll also take a few minutes during announcements next Sunday to bring the congregation up to date. During staff meetings we've talked about it. Staff started out dragging their feet, but they've made an amazing turn-around."

"Pastor, are you ready yet to move ahead with the last piece of this puzzle?"

"Not yet! But we're close. Let's keep it between you and me until the time is right." T paused to sit at his desk. "Are you sure you want to do this?"

Van responded emphatically, "Absolutely. I've never been more certain. Well, let me know—see you soon."

The moment T placed his cell back in his pocket, the phone rang again. He looked at the display to see it was Luke. T's first thought was, "Something went wrong!"

"Hey, Luke, do you have good news or bad news?"

"Great comment! You caught me off guard. I guess a little of both, but mostly good."

"I don't want bad news. Give that to me quickly so it doesn't hurt as much."

"Okay! I'm a jerk and not a very good Christian!"

"Luke, in itself, that's bad, but I don't believe it's that bad. Give me more."

"Well, Pastor, your friend JJ, who I called a street bum, was at the Coffee Grounds Café this morning. I finished my coffee, and I deliberately looked the other way as I headed for the door to leave the café.

"As I walked by his table, he turned and said, 'Hey, man! Are you a friend of the Pastor T dude? I almost told him that I didn't appreciate his being disrespectful by calling you 'dude.'"

"That's his language, Luke. Continue!"

"When I answered 'yes' with some hesitation in my voice, he asked me if you're for real. At that point I didn't know what to think, but something told me I should play this thing out. I asked if I could sit down and—"

Interrupting Luke, T asked, "Is that the bad news? If it is, I can handle it!"

"Yes, that's the bad news. I'm especially embarrassed at my judgmental attitude. That wasn't very Godly! I have such a different impression of JJ now that we talked. He thinks you walk on water, but he had to be reassured that you were authentic. JJ is not a church advocate, but he's not the person I perceived him to be, either."

"I'm so glad the two of you met. He's the kind of person Jesus would hang out with. When you get to know him better, the two of you could be very good friends."

"Right! How could I be so stupid and disrespectful? Also arrogant! If I put my foot in my mouth again, please slam the door on my head!"

"It'll be my pleasure! We all have our bad days. Yes, you messed up, but God has already forgiven you—now, forgive yourself. Hey, are we going to see you Monday at the Disciples Group breakfast?"

"I guess I need some mentoring. Yes, I'll be there!"

Pastor spent the rest of the morning in a couple short meetings. It was time to meet JJ at noon. T wanted to get there before Lil in case JJ showed up early. He grabbed a folder and hit the sidewalk heading toward the Village.

As he got to the Village, he looked at his watch. The sparkle of the diamond at twelve o'clock again brought memories of his dad saying, "Son, God will not let you down!" The anticipation of this meeting with JJ was something T was not taking for granted. His thoughts went to JJ, and he tried to discern if he was pushing too hard and if JJ would revert to his previous life. T had something to propose to JJ, but was it the right time?

As he walked further down the street, he saw JJ walking toward the Coffee Grounds Café. T waved and motioned JJ to meet him in the park across the street. JJ responded with a "thumbs-up." Both arrived at the park entrance about the same time.

"Hey, my friend!" Pastor butted fists with JJ. "You look relaxed today!"

"I am, but I'm always a bit tight when you're pitching." Smiling admirably, JJ continued, "You have that mean off-speed pitch, and I'm a fast-ball hitter."

"JJ, I do have a mean change-up today—watch your balance!" They both enjoyed the humor. "Let's find a picnic table."

"You having lunch catered, Pastor?" Looking at T's grin, JJ exclaimed, "Man, you are! Is that your off-speed pitch?"

"That's one of my pitches—and you went after it! I do have a surprise. My wife, Lil, wants to meet you. She's bringing us a picnic lunch. I hope that's okay with you."

"Hey, you're kidding. Man, there is something going down here or you wouldn't bring in the General."

"She just pulled into the parking lot, JJ. Come and help me with the food."

JJ and T hurried over as Lil parked the Silver Streak. She got out of the car as T introduced JJ. Lil gave JJ a high five and said,

"JJ, wonderful meeting you. You are a household name in our home. Has T set the hook yet?"

"Come on, that's my line! Your husband cast his line, but he can't hook me alone—isn't that why you're here?"

All three of them laughed. It was obvious JJ was a little uncomfortable with all the attention. They carried the basket and soft drinks directly to the picnic table, and Lil pulled out a table cloth.

"Ma'am, this is the strangest moment of my life. I've never been on a picnic. It's like something out of a movie. You did this for me? Why all the fuss?"

"Because you're special! God has big plans for you."

"Yeah, you're the General all right. I asked Pastor Dude why he was bringing in more troops. Something bad always happens when I get outnumbered."

Finishing setting everything on the table, Lil said, "Not today, dude! I'm just a back-up if the pastor can't reel you in."

"Man, Pastor T, the General is something else. She speaks my language."

"I think that means you're comfortable. Are you ready to eat?" Pastor T asked JJ if he would pray.

"Nah, you know the words."

Lil volunteered, "Lord, heavenly Father..."

Lil finished a short prayer in which she thanked God for His many blessings including bringing JJ into their lives. JJ was obviously touched, but he acted as though it didn't affect him. They talked all the way through the meal. Lil was the conversationalist and asked JJ a lot of questions. As they finished JJ tried to find some words to thank her for the lunch but also to let her know that he liked her.

"Hey, Pastor Dude, does the General always ask this many questions?" 2J inquired. "You're much nicer than the street cops, but in street life they're the only ones who ask this many questions—and they never brought a picnic lunch."

"JJ, I heard you met Luke this morning!"

"Yeah, I almost had to trip him to get his attention, but I had to do a background check on you. Man, how did you know?"

"He called to tell me he enjoyed meeting you."

"For real? He was pretty cautious at first—like I was going to pull a blade. He probably grew up with a silver spoon in his mouth. He really said he enjoyed our talk?"

"Yes, on the Bible—that's the truth. He also said he wants to get to know you better."

"Yeah, sure! People like him feel contaminated around people like me. Man, they go to the other side of the street so they don't have to pass me on the sidewalk. I won't see him again."

"Never say never! You might be pleasantly surprised."

"Hey, you two," Lil said, "carry the stuff back to the car and I'll leave you to your business."

"What business? I thought this was lunch and good-bye." JJ looked at his bare wrist as though he had a watch. He looked up with a deceptive grin on his face. "Dude, you know how busy my schedule is."

"Grab a basket, JJ. I know your schedule is full all afternoon, but I want another forty-five minutes. Can you spare the time?"

"Man, I'll check with my office!" JJ glanced at the palm of his hand and then looked up and said, "I just cancelled my one o'clock appointment."

"Great! Let's get the General on her way, and we can get serious."

Adding humor but still demonstrating caution, JJ said, "Uh, oh: do I need an attorney?"

In the parking lot they got the Silver Streak loaded for Lil. JJ acted uncomfortable about saying his good-byes to Lil. He poked his head in the open window of the passenger side of the car, saying,

"Did the pastor dude put you up to this today?"

"No, JJ! It was my idea—in fact, Pastor was concerned that I might scare you off." Leaning slightly toward JJ, Lil admitted, "It felt good to do it, JJ. God probably gave me the idea." Grabbing JJ's arm, she continued, "My husband has talked so fondly of you, I consider you part of our family—I just had to meet you. Now I can see why Pastor can't stop talking about you."

"General, this was my first picnic ever!" Very nervous about what he should say next, he stammered, "I—I didn't know there were people like the two of you. You mean you did this just because? I owe you nothing?"

"Just because, JJ! We love you! Have a good day."

"Gracias, amiga—I mean General!"

Pastor was surprised, "Do you speak Spanish, JJ?"

"Oh, it's just Spanish that I learned from King. Didn't I tell you that his father was from Mexico? He always called me "mi hermano de la calle." I learned later it meant "my street brother." Anyway, learning his language helped me to survive on the streets. It comes in handy even now. Some of my friends don't dig good English yet. I guess I have a lot to learn about both languages."

"You amaze me!" The two of them waved good-bye to Lil as she exited the parking lot.

"Come on, it's no big deal! Now what do you have in mind? Remember, I cancelled all my appointments," JJ grinned.

"I want to walk you past a building in the Village."

"I don't get it, dude! We're going to walk past a building?"

"Yes! But first, did you contact any wholesale suppliers for your business?"

"Yeah, I located one only three blocks from here that's in the warehouse district. They discount the retail price by fifty percent and in some cases even more. I did walk down there just to see if it was for real. They gave me a tour and asked if I wanted to open an account."

"What did you tell them?"

"Well, dude, I told them that I'd do it later. Everything will be cash for the first two months, but after that they said they'll give me credit to pay monthly with an additional ten percent discount, if I pay on time."

"That's great! Last time we talked about a need for a cell phone as your primary business number."

"Yo, I did check into that with about three providers. It looks like even the best rate is not in my pocketbook until I have some income coming in. Why are you doing this, Pastor? It's just a dream."

"Maybe! Maybe not!" Van's building was right in front of them, and JJ hadn't suspected anything yet. "Stop! Look around, JJ, and tell me what you see."

"Dude, are you playing games? Man, I see a busy street, the college up the hill, some businesses, people walking by, and a building with a sign, *As We Go Ministries*. Oh, I get it! The pastor dude is starting a church in the Village, right here, in this building, and he has some weird idea that he is going to get me in it.

"I figured you out! When you failed to get me interested in going to your church, you brought the mountain to me. Right? I'm on to you!"

"Slow down, JJ! No, you're not right. Have I ever put pressure on you to go to my church?"

"No! But it isn't coincidence that we are standing in front of a building with a 'ministry' sign on it. Or did God just put the sign up?"

"You're right, JJ! It's no coincidence! But, for a street person, you're not very observant. Think about our conversation all the way down here."

"Dude, you asked questions about my business dream to have a music repair shop someday." JJ paused and looked around. "Wait a minute! Are you saying this is a good location for a man cave? You are way out of my pockets now!"

"Let's walk across the street and sit on the bench as you look back at this building. It's a little complicated, and it's something that's not ready to fly yet, but it has potential."

"Man, why do I have the feeling that I'm being flipped by the Dude and the General?"

Smiling at JJ's suspicious attitude, T responded, "That's why I like you, JJ—you're a constant challenge! But you're intelligent, you're willing to work hard, you like to make people happy, and I believe you have a bigger faith in Jesus than you want people to think. Do you trust me?"

"More than I do anyone I know. Pastor Dude, I just don't want to get duped by the one I trust. Go ahead and explain, because I know you have some complex plan and I'm in it!"

"You got me there! Okay, are you ready to listen? I take that back! Listen, even if you're not ready. Here's the story. One of the members of my congregation who knows of you from the last two weekend messages I delivered owns this building. About a month ago I started networking with some other young people in the Village..."

Pastor T told JJ the entire story about how *As We Go Ministries* got started and was scheduled to have its first meeting in a week and a half. He explained that Luke was selected to chair the council along with Todd, Leah, Van, and Dan.

"JJ, you met Luke this morning. I didn't know anything about that meeting until Luke called me and said that you're a regular guy. In fact, you initiated that meeting with him. Was that God working?"

"Touché! You got me. I don't have a clue what is real anymore. God has been in my head a lot lately. Man, why doesn't he speak my language so I know what He's thinking? Did Luke really say I was a regular guy?"

"Yes, in so many words. Luke called me to eat a little crow. He confessed that he had previously pictured you differently. But let me continue. You are not being asked to be a part of this servanthood project. Up until now, it was completely separate from the reason I brought you down here."

"Why do you say, 'Up until now'?"

"JJ, God opened a new opportunity when you said you spoke and understood Spanish. I don't think either of us understands what God's drumming up. But I feel it's something more awesome than our minds have visualized. In some way, God will use your music talents and interest in people. For now let's keep it simple."

"Hey, I'm all for simple! So why did you bring me down here?"

"You heard me say that Van owns this building. Well, he'd like to help you get started in business. Being a successful businessperson himself, he has a lot to offer a young person like you, if you have an open mind to learn from him."

"Of course, but advice without—well, you know my resources. The only things I have in my pocket are holes. How is this supposed to happen? I think you know I'll do anything, but there ain't no free lunch."

"JJ, take another look at this building."

"It's a good-looking building with great exposure to the street traffic. It has parking. What am I supposed to see?"

"Look to the left of the *As We Go Ministries* room."

"It looks like a separate office or something. No, no! Man, this can't be! Are you saying this Van guy wants to rent me that space for a music repair business?"

"Yes and no! Yes, Van has the space available and would like to talk with you. No, it isn't exactly a rental right away—maybe more of an investment. Tell me, JJ, can you visualize managing your music repair business in that space?"

"Man, I've got to pinch myself. Am I awake—did you say that it's possible? It's perfect! Let me catch my breath! What's the catch?"

"Have you heard the Eastern proverb, 'Give a man a fish, you feed him for a day; teach him to fish, you feed him for a lifetime'?"

"Not really! It makes sense, though—Van would rather teach me the ropes of business so I can be successful instead of handing it to me on a platter and maybe watching me fail."

"JJ, you're good with words! You're so insightful. I can't give you the details, but there's potential to make something happen. He asked me this morning if you're ready to go, and I said, 'not yet!' That's what I had in my back pocket for you today. Are you ready?"

"Am I ready? Man, you have no idea how ready! But it still sounds like a con. I want to know what I'm getting into!"

"You didn't hear me! It's an investment! It'll be an investment for Van, and it'll be an investment for you. The two of you will have to talk and work it out. How about tomorrow afternoon at 1:30?"

"Dude, you must wear out a pair of sneakers every month. Nothing grows under your feet. Will you be there?"

"I can be, but it might be better if you meet with Van by yourself. He could meet you right here and give you a tour of the building and review the terms. Later it can be put in writing, and the two of you will sign it as a legal binding contract.

"The thing you must understand is that Van wants to do this as a Christian who likes to give young people a chance to succeed. I didn't twist his arm. He feels, if given the opportunity, you will respond to his love and God's love by helping others in a Godly way."

"Pastor Dude, will you still be around? Or is this your way of bailing?"

"You're my friend! I'm not going to bail. Oh, I have a small group of people coming to my house on Sunday evening. I want you to meet them. In fact, I pray you'll share your story with them."

"Still trolling!" JJ was grinning from ear to ear. "You've worked on me so long that I'm worn out. I'd rather face a gang with chains, but if you want me there, I'll do it. Dude, I guess that says that I trust you will not let me embarrass myself."

"Gracías, amigo! See you at 6 p.m. Oh, will you consider dropping in a week from next Wednesday night for the first session of *As We Go Ministries?*"

"Don't push it, Pastor Dude!" The two had a good laugh, butted fists, and headed their own ways.

LOOKING FOR MEANING:

1. Can you think of a time when you misjudged someone and had to eat crow later?

2. Why do you think it was so easy for Lil to create a relationship with JJ?

3. From some of the comments JJ made to Pastor T, what do you think is going through his mind?

Chapter 12—Tell Your Story!

"So the man went away and began to tell in the Decapolis how much Jesus had done for him. And all the people were amazed."
Mark 5:20 *(NIV)*

Jesus had just removed the unclean spirits from a man who was demon possessed. Jesus then instructed the man to tell! Jesus expects us to tell our story to others.

Chapter 12 illustrates the impact of one person telling his story of how he learned of Christ.

Tell Your Story!

Pastor and JJ had clearly become good friends, and JJ was starting to trust T. Pastor had also been in contact with Oz, Liz, and Vi to discuss their respective situations and had followed up on the idea to bring them all together. His wife, Lil, was wondering how he was going to pull it off because they were all so diverse. So T had been praying the Lord would bless the gathering and somehow pull them together in the unity of Christ.

It was just after their evening meal on Friday. Pastor T was in his home study as Lil brought him a cup of coffee.

"Thank you, Lil. That hazelnut coffee smells so good. By the way, I contacted everyone earlier this week with an invite to our house on Sunday evening. Today JJ indicated he'd come also. Are you still okay with this small group?"

"As long as I don't have to be a special-order cook. How about you firing up the grill and I'll do something with veggies?"

"Sounds great! We can eat on the patio."

"That's fine. Did you request an RSVP so I can plan the food?"

"Sorry, I didn't ask for a firm commitment. Everyone sounded like they were going to make it. Vi's husband, Tom, may be on call at the hospital but will try to be here. You're still concerned, aren't you?"

"Sort of! We've never entertained such a diverse group. I don't know how you're going to bring them together so they relate to one another."

"I'm not! That's God's job. I just know He will. I'm guessing God has a pleasant surprise for us and He may use JJ to unite the group."

"I know God does wonderful things, but uniting a doctor, a community leader, a corporate executive, a truck driver, and a kid from the streets would be a miracle. That's not even counting the surprise you've arranged. Can you pull that off?"

"That's what God does best—it's in His hands now. We've taken what we think is appropriate action. Now it will be God who will intervene with His action."

"Praise the Lord! And T, thank you for sharing JJ at the picnic. He is so—" Interrupting Lil, her husband asked, "—likable?"

"Yes, but more than that, JJ is magnetic. He has a type of charm that attracted me and made me really comfortable. He also has a mystique about him that makes me want to befriend him."

"Well, JJ took to you immediately. Your picnic idea was a winner!"

On Saturday afternoon T received a call from Van about his meeting with JJ. He told T that he was impressed with JJ's willingness to learn and his knowledge of the technical end of instrument repair. Van referred to JJ's personality as "contagious."

They reviewed the relationship and the process for getting the business going but intentionally hadn't agreed on anything yet. That was because Van requested that each of them pray and meditate on this relationship before making a final decision. Van said he was surprised that JJ was willing to approach God and request direction on this decision. Van also explained the concept of a marketplace ministry but didn't attach any requirement.

The two of them agreed to meet again Monday morning to discuss how God responded to their prayers. At that time they would discuss a written agreement. JJ asked Van how to listen to

God. They had a good discussion about how God might plant a thought in your mind or you wake up in the morning and suddenly you have the solution to a question you were pondering the night before. Van told JJ that he asks questions of God and meditates to see what visual images He plants in his mind. Sometimes it's a feeling you just can't shake.

After talking to Van, Pastor T finalized his message for Sunday. It was to be entitled, "God is 3D!" He walked into the kitchen, and Lil said, "I made fresh coffee—want some?"

"You read my mind. Lil, I got an idea."

"So, what's new? Your mind never shuts down. Want to talk about it?"

"Yeah, let's go out on the patio. I need you to brainstorm with me."

"Why not? Here's a platter of cookies I bought at the church cookie sale this morning."

"The beauty of the outdoors is so relaxing. Lil, for the past week I've been feeling that we haven't thought of everything for JJ's business adventure. Van is doing a fantastic job, and from the business point of view, he's right on. He's so good at putting all the pieces together. Van's a strategic leader. This morning it came to me, like God just said, 'Consider this!'"

Lil responded, "I'm listening."

Placing his mug on the table, T continued, "There has to be a ministry opportunity here someplace. God must intend that JJ is a key player in a bigger concept. I don't want to rush it, but I can't stop thinking about it. Lil, give me an off-the-wall concept. You're good at that."

"Okay!" With her hand to her chin, she thought for a few seconds, took a deep breath, and began, "How about combining the two concepts of music instrument repair and *As We Go Ministries* into one ministry with two dimensions. Open the bigger room that you're only using one night a week for music lessons, music events, exercise, small groups, etc. JJ could be responsible as caretaker of the building. JJ could even start a transitional ministry in the open area where people from the streets come to a Christ-centered support group to help them transition into a job and find housing, etc. It could even be used for a soup kitchen sponsored by our people at church. It would be a good opportunity for our people to get missional—get them out of the church to serve.

"Maybe we're thinking way too small. It could be a church plant that's community based and nontraditional. It could also be used as a town hall gathering place in the Village to discuss issues, conduct debates, even teach Christian-based classes approved and accredited by the college. Why not sponsor English as a Second Language opportunity for Hispanics who don't have the privilege of going to college? That's a perfect fit with JJ knowing Spanish. It's possible that some of these people have not finished high school and could get a GED right there. I also—"

"Take a breath!" T interrupted. "Wow, I really like your ability to get off-the-wall ideas. Some things may seem unrealistic right now, but you struck a chord, Lil—introduce a bigger concept. I like it! I think that is what God was trying to tell me. We need one statement, not a bunch of little ones. We can plant the seed so it has the potential to be multi-dimensional. That gives God the latitude to make it grow in His time frame."

"Will your Village people buy into that? Or are they already protecting their turf?"

"I think we're okay there—we have to start somewhere! I'll talk to Van, and he'll have an idea on the approach. The council can still be the operational board. We have to find a way that allows JJ to grow and, eventually, expand his ministry. Right now he doesn't see it as a ministry."

"Can you turn your switch off and just enjoy this beautiful day?" Lil grabbed T's hand as they settled in their lounge chairs and stared up into the sky.

Sunday was a big day as Pastor T wrapped up the last of the topical series on being missional. He also introduced the Village ministry concept. He decided to cast that vision as part of his message.

Pastor saw the get-together at his house as a form of worship—not just a social event. It was an opportunity for God to come into the hearts of those attending and then up to the group to respond to God's love.

Everyone had confirmed they would come. JJ was most hesitant because he was nervous about people not accepting him. That night T fired up the grill and had hamburgers ready to throw on as the people started to arrive. Lil worked inside on a vegetable mixture with some special seasoning. She also wanted to surprise them with her favorite dessert, chocolate éclairs.

JJ was the first to show, and the rest came shortly after. T guided them to the table with beverages and some finger snacks while he did the grill thing. He introduced everyone and made the rounds until the burgers were done.

"I hate to break up this lively fellowship," Pastor shouted, then lowered his voice. "I'd like to ask God to join us and provide His blessing over our get-together." T proceeded to pray.

Lil made everyone feel comfortable with her hospitality. "Everyone just sit around the table while Pastor and I serve the food. Please continue your conversations and enjoy the evening."

Following a lot of talking and people patting their full stomachs, Lil brought out a full platter of chocolate éclairs along with hazelnut coffee.

"Lil, you are the most gracious host," responded Liz politely. "I have never had a dessert and coffee combination this good."

"Beats the truck stops I eat in!" remarked Oz. "Great burgers, Pastor."

"Thanks everyone! It's been my privilege to have all of you in my life. This is probably as diverse a group as we have ever entertained—and you've hit it off remarkably well. I've prayed for this moment, and by God's grace He has placed each of you here this evening. Each of us is unique with a different background, lifestyle, and interest. One thing we all share is a desire to grow in Christ.

"There isn't a person here who doesn't have a story to share, but tonight I've asked JJ, or as he sometimes prefers, 2J, to share his story. I met JJ..." Pastor T told how they met and a few things about the subsequent meetings and then said, "I'll just turn it over to JJ."

Standing nervously and rubbing his hands together, JJ proceeded with caution, "Pastor T and I met accidentally—at least that is what I thought a few months ago. Since then I've come to believe that God set this whole thing up. This is something I don't want to do. My story's nothing special where I come from, and there's no way I can find the right words to express myself. I worried about this all week, but finally Pastor T said to just be myself. That's the only way I know, so I hope you put up with my street manners.

"The pastor dude," he said looking at Pastor, "is like a bull dog. He just won't give up. He had his teeth in my pant leg from the moment we met. It's strange though: I acted like I wasn't interested and brushed him off several times, but in my gut I was hoping he wouldn't let go. Man, with what seemed like twenty thousand questions about me and my life, I felt safe enough to pull out some bad memories and share them with Pastor Dude. I can't think of one reason why any of you would be interested in a street bum, gang member, someone who stole to survive, and someone who was conditioned to fight or be killed, but maybe with the dude holding me up, I'll make it through.

"I'll start with my parents. Man, when they weren't drunk or high, they were good to me. We lived in a rat-infested apartment. They were gone a lot, so I fended for myself. There was a neighbor kid down the hall five years older than me. He was like a brother and, yeah, even a parent at times. I always called him King Dude. He picked up the handle 'King' because he hung out at Burger King. His real name was José, but everyone had nick names, and I never did learn his last name.

"I was eight years old and we were playing stickball in the street in front of our apartment one night and the cops pulled up in a black and white. Man, we started to scatter because when cops show up, they're looking for somebody. That night they were looking for me, but not because I was in trouble. This one cool cop named Thump—at least that's what we called him—collared me as I was running away. The King saw this while he was running and came back. King was yelling at the cop that I hadn't done anything. Thump sat us both down on the curb and told us that my parents were in a car crash and they were both dead. Thump asked if I had any relatives. I told him my mom and dad never talked about relatives.

"The King jumped in and said he would take care of me. Thump took me in the black and white, which I thought was cool. But he told me somebody from county was going to put me someplace. A woman picked me up and took me to a place where there were like twenty beds in one room. Someone took me to the funeral, but we were the only people there. Some guy said a few words about my parents and then came over to me and gave me a hug. I smelled the booze on him, so he must a been some friend of my parents.

"That night I snuck out of the place I was staying, ran across town, and found my friend King. He had just been in a street fight and some really bad guys were looking for him. We decided to leave the neighborhood.   Pastor, this is really bad—you want me to chill?"

"JJ, do you see anyone leaving?"

"Oh, please continue, JJ!" Vi pleaded. "We want to hear it all."

"Well, okay—the King and I spent most of our first night running and walking. I finally ran out of gas and fell asleep in some alley with a bunch of garbage dumpsters. When I woke up, I was hungry. King had already dug through the dumpsters, and we had bananas and sour milk. I remember being cold, and King lifted a jacket out of one of the rummage stores. It seemed exciting at first. Man, it was the King and me! We then found out what the streets were like, but I was lucky because King always watched my back."

JJ's story covered eleven years on the streets, King's violent death, his own near-death experience, and his journey with music leading him out of the streets. He explained that music kept him alive as he played on street corners for a few coins. He finally got into a band and shared an apartment with one of the band members. Odd jobs and band gigs helped him to start a band of his own. Everyone in the group had their eyes glued on JJ as their jaws almost touched the patio table from his stories.

Lil leaned over and whispered into T's ear, "It looks like your surprise isn't going to show!" T responded with a shrug of his shoulders, meaning, "I don't know!"

"JJ," Pastor asked, "what was your lowest moment on the streets?"

"Oh, man—you may think that it was when I lost my parents, or when King was killed, or maybe even as I faced my Maker with a blade at my throat, but it wasn't. You have to realize that I missed out on nine years of school during that time. I didn't miss that until I started to realize that I was living in the bottom of the barrel. Most of my acquaintances on the streets couldn't spell their own name or read anything except the graffiti in front of their nose. It really scared me because I didn't want to live on the streets forever. I'm still self-conscious when I talk—like tonight. I feel you're keeping track of all my stupid speaking errors.

"To answer Pastor Dude's question, I was about fourteen or fifteen when I met this bum in the park. He was in his fifties, and I got to know him because we shared the same fire barrel and I would hang out in the park. He was a wino, but he had been a teacher in some private school. He asked me the question, 'Kid, do you want to get out of here?' I really didn't want him to think I wanted out, because that would make me different. And that's dangerous on the streets. So I said, 'Nah, it's a good life!'

"This bum was called 'Professor.' The professor looked at me and smiled with his yellow and black decayed teeth and said, 'Okay, kid, here's to your future. You can be just like me!' He chug-a-lugged the rest of his bottle and passed out with his head on a picnic table. He was drooling on his shirt sleeve and he stunk to high heaven.

"I spent the night in a storm sewer culvert to keep warm. I was sitting with my head between my legs thinking that this was going to be my life. I cried until there were no more tears left. I threw up so hard I could hardly catch my breath. I had never felt so lonely and so trapped in all my life. I didn't sleep all night. I listened to the fighting and swearing that echoed through the sewer tunnels. At that point I knew exactly why some end their misery by jumping in front of a train.

"In the morning I crawled out of the sewer culvert and found a dumpster. I saw some bananas and was reminded of the first morning when King brought sour milk and bananas. I got the dry heaves from the thought. I couldn't eat—it all looked like garbage to me.

"I wandered to the park to get some fresh air. I had the stink from many nights without a bath, and I could even smell my own terrible breath. The Professor was sitting by the same table. He saw me and waved me over. I felt sick again just thinking about getting close to him. He yelled, 'Hey, kid, I got something for you.' I reluctantly went toward him. He was waving a book in his hand, saying, 'Kid, this is your ticket out!' He handed me this book called *Oliver Twist*[6] by Charles Dickens.

"It meant nothing to me. He said to read it—no, he said, 'You idiot, read it, and when you finish come back and get another one. You can read, can't you?' I nodded my head yes. Problem was, I couldn't read very good. There was this shelter where street folks would come at night to sleep. During the day it was pretty quiet. The front porch was perfect! I read there each day for a week. This Dickens guy captured me with his good-versus-evil writing style. At first I thought that the Professor meant that this one book was my ticket off the streets, but I learned that he meant I should develop my reading skills and benefit from some of the reading material he had. Over the next year my reading improved as he kept giving me one book after another. He would often ask me questions about the book, and we would sit all afternoon discussing the content.

"I don't know where he got all the books; I never asked. I sort of think he still had connections with a nearby library. One day about a year later I found him slumped over the same picnic bench, dead. He was bleeding from the mouth with an empty whisky bottle on the ground. There was a book on the table. It was *The Christmas Carol* [7] by Charles Dickens. I knew it was for me and it would be my last book from the Professor. He led me out of the darkest part of my life with the only thing he could give me, his books and his wisdom.

"I suppose you're thinking that God came to me and pulled me up by my boot straps to break away from that life. Looking back, it's pretty easy to see that God had his DNA all over the sequence of events, but remember I had no clue that God was around. In fact, I thought God had given up and deserted me. I didn't see the King, the Professor, or even the Priest who saved my life as guardian angels, except that they each had a big heart.

"So there you have it! Pretty ordinary, right!" Silence prevailed. "Pastor Dude, do you want me to exit now? I really feel uncomfortable."

Vi, so touched by JJ's life, firmly said, "Absolutely not! JJ, are you thinking we don't want you here? That was an incredible story." She cleared her throat. "Pardon me, but you brought me right to my knees. Right now, I'm all choked up and fighting tears of joy."

"Hey, you guys, I don't want you to feel sorry for me."

"It's not that, JJ," Liz said. "We're filled with emotion out of respect for you. How you came from despair to where you are now. You just took us on the ride of our lives. All the times I have been stressed out because my fingernail broke or because someone forgot my birthday—2J, I am truly humbled by you and God. I would be honored if you'd consider me your friend."

"I've experienced a lot as a truck driver," Oz added, "but you just taught me something I'll never, ever let go of—the value of my family and friends. JJ, welcome to the other side of the world. Pastor told us about you in Sunday worship, but it wasn't until this moment that I found a new type of relationship with my God. I think it's called, 'Prove that you can love one another, and I will know that you love Me.' Those are not the exact words, but it fits what I feel right now."

Pastor interjected, "JJ hasn't even touched on the best part, but first I have a surprise." Lil looked up, wondering what was going on. She knew about the surprise but had no idea T had it just inside the house.

"JJ, this surprise is for you. Remember when you almost had your throat cut and this big dude got you and King to the hospital?"

"Yeah? We called him 'One Punch' because he had been a professional boxer! He saved our lives! I remember he called me 'Spider' because I was all arms and legs."

Pastor T updated everyone on the story, opened the sliding-glass door, and introduced One Punch. A guy about 6' 4", with gray hair and in great physical condition, ducked under the top of the door opening and headed for JJ. They embraced and pretended to throw a few punches.

JJ was completely surprised. "This isn't real! Do you still have your gym? Man, you were my mentor! You saved my life!"

"Spider! I love you, man! Yeah, I have the gym and, by the way, kid, you owe me for busting my lip. You're the only white kid that had lead in his knuckles!"

"I remember—lucky punch!"

Pastor asked One Punch to recall his experience with JJ for the group. One Punch was colorful, using his fists as he was talking. When he finished, Pastor invited him to stay. Lil brought out her chocolate éclairs with the hazelnut coffee and served One Punch.

Pastor T wanted the group to hear one more thing. "JJ, let's get back to the part you didn't cover."

"Pastor Dude and One Punch are a lot alike. They're relentless! I think the part T is talking about is his trolling for sinners in the Village. I put up a good fight, but he sorta hooked me. Seriously, I wasn't looking for God, and I didn't want God or any relationship in my life. That's when Pastor T started casting his salvation lure. I consider myself a street-smart dude who can survive all by himself. I didn't want anybody messing me up. But the T dude messed me up!

"I found a friend, just like One Punch, who didn't put me down or try to take advantage of me. He strong-armed me to look at a different life—life with Jesus. I can't say that I am ready for church and all that stuff, but I feel different, and I find myself asking, 'What would Jesus do?' The problem is, I don't have a clue what Jesus would do—I don't even have a Bible. I frankly don't like church music, and I dread the thought of going to church—probably because I've only been there once in my life. My life is more messed up right now than it ever has been.

"One Punch, do you have an opening in your gym?" Everyone laughed. "I don't know how to react to something I can't touch or see. I told Pastor Dude that I want to give it a chance. He calls that discipleship—he explained it as growing in Christ. Pastor also put a twist on my growing in Christ. I thought that was it, but he said that as I grow, I have to grow others. He called it 'making disciples.' I know only one thing—I miss being wanted or needed. The King gave that to me for a long time. No promises, but I will try to understand the God T has talked so much about."

"Amen, bro!" One Punch celebrated the moment, "Go, Spider!"

"JJ, I'm a doctor, and I've seen what life on the streets can produce," said Tom. "Our ER can sew them up and give the right injection, but we keep sending them back to the streets. You and One Punch have brought a new dimension to my thinking this evening. If we as a group stick together, strengthen our relationship, grow together in Christ—we can make a difference. Maybe it's possible to work with One Punch and help kids through some kind of small-group ministry. We've had a great time together tonight. I'm serious about continuing to meet. I want to have some impact outside the operating room in a hospital."

Ags, stumbling for the right words, confided, "JJ, I'm really quiet and don't usually say much. You've made me realize that I should thank God ten times a day for all He's given our family. We struggle to make ends meet, but now I know we are rich in the blessings God has given to Oz, me, and our children. Let's keep meeting and, JJ, we need you in the group."

Liz spoke up. "JJ, I'm a single parent who fell into the trap of isolating myself from all relationships and making my career my haven. Pastor T has helped me to start reprioritizing my life, but you clinched it tonight. I'll arrange my schedule so I can meet weekly if that is what everyone wants—you just name the day, time, and place. I've been self-centered far too long—I want to make an impact inside and outside my corporate office."

"Tom and I have been talking about setting one evening aside for the sake of our relationship. We were talking about Thursdays—does that work for everyone?" asked Vi.

"You dudes are great, but I don't know if I can fit it in my schedule—just kidding! I want to tell each of you that for the first time ever, I feel like my life has hope. Thanks all of you for making me feel comfortable—thank you, God, for..." JJ choked as his eyes watered.

Everyone in the room rushed to JJ and gave him a hug and continued to embrace each other. Wet eyes were prevalent, but no one cared. Lil worked herself to the middle of the group and approached JJ with a Bible in her hand.

"JJ, this is for you." She handed the Bible to JJ. "Use it with God's love."

Feeling compelled to set the next gathering, Oz said, "Hey, everyone, we have a small home, but you're invited to start our small group in our house a week from Thursday at 5:30. I'll throw some hot dogs on the grill. One Punch, can we keep in touch? You and your gym ministry are helping a lot of kids. Ags and I would like to help. As Tom mentioned, maybe our group can do something."

"JJ, bring your guitar," Liz suggested. "Maybe teach us a song or two. Give it to us your way!"

"Hey, Spider, you made me proud! I thought it would be with your fists or guitar, but you actually got some brains!"

"I owe you, man!" responded JJ. "Stick around so we can talk."

Pastor found himself pumping his arms and repeatedly whispering "Thank you, God! Thank you! Amen!"

Later, T and Lil sat outside sharing their thoughts on the get-together. T was excited over the relationships that appeared to be developing and that One Punch brought a missional opportunity to the table that hadn't even been a speculation before.

Lil couldn't get out of her mind how JJ held everyone spellbound with his story. The amazing thing to her was that he remained so poised and humble. Starting to use God for guidance in his life was also rewarding to Lil. They talked for hours. In fact, T couldn't get tired, so he remained on the patio after Lil retired, trying to unwind.

Pastor kept talking to God, thanking and praising Him. Several times he looked up at the sky and asked, "What's next God?—I can't wait to find out."

LOOKING FOR MEANING:

1. What did you find compelling about JJ's story?

2. JJ told about his relationship with God. How would you describe or explain your relationship with God to someone else?

3. How did the events of the evening impact you?

Chapter 13—Intentional!

"It's in Christ that we find out who we are and what we are living for. Long before we first heard of Christ and got our hopes up, he had his eye on us, had designs on us for glorious living, part of the overall purpose he is working out in everything and everyone."
Ephesians 1:11–12 *(Message)*

The Apostle Paul illustrates how intentionally God energizes all believers with the power necessary for spiritual completion.

Chapter 13 shows us how intentionally Pastor T proceeds using as his vision Jesus' command to make disciples.

Intentional!

Lil rolled T out of bed the next morning for his Disciples Group meeting. He kissed her good-bye and was off and running. When he arrived at church, some of the men were already in the kitchen preparing breakfast. Pastor had assigned devotions and discussion leaders for the next twelve meetings.

Today's devotion was John 6:26-27 where Jesus addressed a crowd who had witnessed His healings and His feeding of the multitudes: "...I tell you the truth, you are looking for me, not because you saw miraculous signs but because you ate the loaves and had your fill. Do not work for food that spoils, but for food that endures to eternal life, which the Son of Man will give you. On him God the Father has placed his seal of approval" *(NIV)*.

Discussion among the disciples centered on how our worldly appetite is motivated by our physical and emotional desires. Although Jesus offers the promise of everlasting life, people see only the satisfaction of the material reward.

Van, Dan, and Mick reported on the Village project. They also asked Luke to talk a little about the *As We Go Ministries* plans. Enthusiasm spread through the group, and the men were soon volunteering to help out in the Village.

After the meeting Pastor T asked Van and Luke to meet with him in his office. Van brought his two colleagues with him so they could take ownership of any decisions that might be made.

"Thanks for coming to my little powwow on our Village project. God has been trying to tell me something. For days I haven't been able to figure it out, but it has something to do with me thinking too shallow."

Laughing, Luke said, "That's difficult to believe! You're the one with all the visions."

"I agree!" echoed Van. "I'm just trying to keep up with you. Isn't our project big enough?"

"'Big enough' is not the issue. Broad enough is what I want to discuss. Are we planning broadly enough right now for an expanding future?"

"I get it!" Van exclaimed. "Are you suggesting a broad-based ministry process that can accommodate other ministries if God presents opportunities in the future?"

"Exactly! We already have a council set up for operational governance of the Wednesday evening gathering. Luke, you and your people have done a great job, and it is ready to launch this Wednesday. In the meantime, Van has been talking to JJ about a music instrument repair business/ministry in the same building. New to all of you is the possibility of another dimension that came up last night." T explained the connection between JJ and One Punch. He also went into the small group's interest in helping the Boxing for Kids program in the inner city. "There's so much ministry opportunity that keeps popping up."

"I see a ton of possibilities from your update," Luke added. "Even the JJ thing with English as a Second Language. By the way, I really like JJ and would be honored to work with him in your broader thinking. My dad often said, 'Grassroots ownership is the key to Godly stewardship.' I think I finally understand what he meant."

An idea popped into Van's head. "We have a great theme in *As We Go Ministries*. Maybe that should be our parent corporation, with all the various ministries interlocking toward one goal—making disciples!"

"Luke, your dad's wisdom may be a beacon as we continue developing team-led ministries. It would be a cell approach, with each cell having a different ministry but all working toward one vision. Van, how would all this change the governance structure?"

"We'd develop and submit nonprofit Articles of Incorporation under one legal name to the Secretary of State. That filing would require that we create a board of directors. The council would govern the volunteer operational activities in the building and report to the board as one of the cell ministries. JJ's business/ministry could be an independent business in which the ministry complies with corporate vision. Other cell ministries you are talking about can function as an arm of the nonprofit but have individual governing boards.

"The building could still be a contract with our church or it could be shifted to the new nonprofit. As we add and interlock ministries, the board of directors would designate how each will be accountable and collaborative without taking away the local ownership. We'll have to decide if this is a 501(c)(3) nonprofit. That's where we deal with the feds."

Luke appreciated the cell ministry concept. "I love it, man. Van, you always make it so workable. You're smokin'. I'm in!"

"You have a God-given ability to turn complexity into simplicity," T complimented Van. "Can you draft something in writing so we're all going in the right direction?"

"No problem!" Van agreed. "I'll also explain to JJ this morning when I meet with him about his vision of the music instrument repair business. I hope he sees his business as a marketplace ministry. He was supposed to pray and listen to God over the weekend. I would like to build in the mission of "making disciples" for anything and everything that evolves as a ministry in this concept. Governance is so much easier when everything has the same focus."

The other two disciples contributed and indicated they were onboard with the decision to function under one umbrella rather than a multitude of independent ministries. Van invited T to the meeting with JJ to help in the trust department. Luke volunteered to invite JJ to the Wednesday night get-together and add some pre-activity music. Van and T left for their meeting with JJ at the Village building.

JJ was waiting by Van's building with a bicycle that Van had found for him.

"Hi, Boss Man," JJ said to Van. "You brought the big guy?"

"Yes, JJ! The big guy needs a lesson or two in how to run a business," Van replied as he unlocked the door.

"Man, I dig it! We can't let his head swell."

Pastor kiddingly said, "Watch out, JJ, or I'll give you the permanent label of 'Spider!'"

"Hey, dude, Spider is not so bad. I was content with Spider because it came from One Punch. Last night was awesome! Thanks, man! Also, tell the General she's awesome.

"I learned something last night: the people who are true friends are like a real family. They are the people who believe in me and like me for who I am. They are not the hundreds of phonies who pretend to like me but would trade me in for a stash of grass in a second. Pastor Dude, you were right there for me last night."

"You're welcome. Great words of wisdom, JJ! Van, would you lead us in prayer?"

"I'd be happy to pray, but JJ has been talking and listening to God this weekend. JJ, would you pray in your own words what's on your heart?"

"Me? You're kidding! Man, I'm just getting used to talking to God with no one else around. No one has told me how to pray!"

Intending to be encouraging, Pastor urged, "You're with friends—remember? We'll not judge you, and I know God is just waiting for you to witness to him what is on your heart."

"Hey, you guys are like the pope to me! I feel so tiny and insignificant. But okay, I'll give it a try, but you better not laugh." JJ buried his head in his hands with a long pause.

"God, You are really new to me. Last night I read about You, God. How You created everything. I started to read in my new Bible. One thing I know is that You've been in my life and I didn't even know it. I feel so embarrassed by that. You could've discarded me a long time ago because of my attitude, but You didn't. You even sent reinforcements with people like Pastor Dude, Boss, and the people last night. God, or maybe I should call You Jesus or Lord, I feel like You are lifting me up—my feet ain't even touching the ground. But I feel safe. I can't ask for anything because You've given me so much. I guess I just want to follow Your lead. I ask that You keep the signals coming. Amen!"

Van placed his hand on JJ's shoulder. "Well done! That wasn't so hard!"

"Was too! You guys have been doing it so long the words just flow. I have to think every word or I would be a flip-flop. That's a person who says one thing and does something else. Pastor, did you catch it?"

"Yes, JJ! I caught it—we have far too many flip-flops. Your prayer was heartfelt and God recognizes your sincerity. Hey, glad you're reading your Bible!"

"I still feel pretty inadequate. What's the agenda today?"

"I asked Pastor to come because I know you trust him and I think he'll start out being a listener. Tell us first, how did the talk with God go?"

"Everything like this is new turf for me, but when you told me that being aware of the things happening in my life was also being a good listener for God, it started making sense. Listening, for me, has always been waiting for words I could hear directly from another person.

"First, Boss told me that reading the Bible and absorbing His Word is my ticket to understanding God's will.

"Second, I did talk to God—a lot! I asked a lot of questions. I stood back, watched, and listened. It was kind of seeing the forest and not focusing on one tree. The things that happened were amazing.

"Boss, we met last Friday morning and you completely floored me with your offer to help me get into business. Maybe the best thing you gave me was your advice to look for and feel God's guidance and answers. I woke up Sunday morning not thinking at all about a business, but about how I could help people. I knew that was God and not my selfish thinking. I kept thinking how fixing instruments would help people or better their lives.

"Then Sunday night came and people were helping me. It came to me in a talk with One Punch that opening myself up, taking a risk leads to lasting relationships. He explained that relationships open a wide window of opportunity to improve our lives.

"Pastor, I guess you showed me that a trusting relationship opens up opportunity to talk about Jesus. I'm not at that level yet, but it makes sense that a business should be based on relationships, too—trusting relationships and trying to help people.

"The wider I opened my eyes, the more I saw God's hand in almost everything that happened over the weekend. Boss, you're right about God. He really does respond to our prayers.

"Last night I experienced a group of people who I want to be close to—not just socially but deep, deep in my life. I still don't know what I have to offer, but I'm convinced God has some notion. The other thing is that I always thought I was dumb. I may not be the smartest bird on the perch, but these last few weeks convinced me there is a place for me and I have the brains to improve and become good at it.

"As far as the business, I've read stuff on planning, finance, marketing, etc., but that isn't who I am. I need help, and the Boss showed up. I'm ready to be your student—I guess that's an apprentice," JJ concluded looking directly at Van, who was momentarily speechless.

"I'm deeply impressed," Van said appreciatively. "You're a smart person, JJ. You'll be able to catch on to the business things. Your attitude is the most important. With your faith growing in God and a heart for serving, you will succeed. Remember, success is not the end result but how you approach each and every challenge in a Godly manner to produce a successful result—it's the process of getting there."

"Boss, I have gone through your checklist of start-up things. One question was, 'What is your destination or vision?' It also said keep it simple and—what's the word?—compelling! I first came up with 'helping people.' Then I changed it to 'serving people.' It's more of a slogan than a vision. What do you think, Pastor Dude?"

"You know what I think! Your insight and willingness to be coached makes me proud. Van, is that the kind of statement you had in mind?"

"It's the perfect blend of what JJ wants to become and how God is going to navigate his actions to get there. It tells a lot about JJ's character and the purpose of the business/ministry.

"Maybe that's our umbrella statement for making disciples. It may turn out to be a core value as we get more into the corporation details. One thing, JJ: I arranged to have your bookkeeping done by the church bookkeeper for now. I don't think you're ready to do it yourself or hire someone to do it."

"Good! My bookkeeping is what I have in my pocket. My financial statement is taking it out of my pocket and showing you."

Van and JJ carefully went over the contract to ensure that JJ would have an affordable start-up and eventually work into a ten percent contribution of the net profit back to the church. JJ agreed to the benchmarks that Van had spelled out in the agreement, including one that would enable JJ to live in the apartment over the main floor instrument repair space after six months of compliance with the contract.

Ministry was a carefully drafted theme in the contract, with plenty of opportunities to expand. The Wednesday night building space was labeled as common property to the *As We Go Ministries, Inc.* JJ felt good about his new challenge.

"I'm not deserving of this. My promise to you and to God is that I will serve people with a loving heart. We'll have to see how it goes. Boss, you totally own me, but your kindness allows me to grow into this venture and the flexibility of paying you back as I can afford to do so. Man, you're something else."

"I'll get all these revisions put into the contract. Next step is to sign the agreement. By next week you can start ordering your basic inventory. The $10,000 loan will cover your ramp-up costs. I know you'll be a good steward."

"JJ, I almost forgot," Pastor added. "Liz wants you to call her about giving her daughter, Joey, private guitar lessons. You can use my cell to call her," T handed his phone to JJ, "but let's pray first."

After the prayer, JJ made his call to set up a time with Liz and Joey. Van and JJ stayed to finalize the agreements and talk over some of the cabinetry requirements for JJ's work area. Satisfied that things were on track, Pastor left to go back to church.

When he walked into his office, Vi was waiting for him. She expressed her joy over the get-together the previous evening. Ministry outside the church was all she could talk about. She and Tom had decided to commit time and money to develop a ministry that would help kids who were on the streets. Their idea was to start with the Boxing for Kids ministry, but in some way to network JJ into it to equip kids to succeed in a life off the streets.

Pastor reviewed the *As We Go Ministries* concept with Vi and suggested that she and Tom discuss their idea with the other members of the small group on Thursday. They agreed that it would be better to engage the entire group than everyone trying to do something different.

As Vi left, Pastor looked at his emails. There were messages from Ags and Liz. They both thanked Pastor and Lil for the small-group get-together. Along the same lines as Vi, they wanted to do something as a group to have an influence outside the church. Pastor responded by suggesting they set time aside on Thursday to talk about a servant group project.

Along with several other emails, there was one from a gentleman in the congregation who was upset about the emphasis on work outside the church. In fact, the guy really ripped into Pastor for using his position to distract from taking care of the church's members. Pastor put his elbows on the desk, using both hands to run his fingers through his hair. He remembered his dad saying, "You aren't there to make everybody happy. You must be true to God." That gave him the courage to call Joe, the man with the complaint. As the phone rang, Pastor T kept wondering what to say. Just then, a guy answered. The voice seemed pleasant enough.

"Good afternoon, Joe! This is Pastor T. I just read your email and thought we should talk."

The tone changed from pleasant to angry. "There's nothing to talk about, Pastor. You need to start servicing your own members and quit using the money we're paying you to run around and befriend no-good drifters."

"I'm so sorry you feel we aren't doing enough for you. Please tell me where you feel we are not doing a good job."

"It's just that! You're telling us that we shouldn't expect anything for ourselves but give everything to people outside the church. That's nonsense! In fact, it's stupid! If you don't serve your own members and make them happy, you'll find yourself without any."

"I'm trying to listen to your complaint, but please remember, we are not deserting our members. We're only trying to give them the opportunity to take on a greater challenge. Mission-based churches have found that serving others is far more fulfilling than just receiving all the benefits of a self-serving church."

"I take exception to your assumptions," Joe replied. "Part of my membership is for presence in the community. I want my family to go to a church that offers meaningful activities and events so people associate me with activity and progress. Not one that imposes itself on the community and gives handouts to dirt bags who refuse to work!"

"If that's your reason for belonging, we really should talk more and discuss the Biblical perspective of your concern," T said. "It seems like a worldly view is clouding your judgment right now."

"There is no cloud in my judgment!" Joe said angrily. "It sounds like you're just writing us off! We should just leave."

"On the contrary, I very much want you to remain in the church. However, our church is the body of Christ. That means Jesus is the head of our church. Growing to be more like Jesus is what we want each person in the church to do. That also means that He wants His church family to be sent into the community and beyond to serve."

"There are many who disagree with you. I'll take my money elsewhere."

"Sir," T said calmly, "if that's your decision, please consider praying about it with your family. God loves you and wants you as part of His family. Anytime you want to talk, I'll make myself available. Money and influence should not be the issue—an open heart to believe and live by the promises given to us by our Lord and Savior is the issue."

A few nasty words later, Joe hung up. T ran his fingers through his hair again, saying, "God, are you testing me? Why is doing the right thing so hard? Why are old paradigms such strong barriers to change?" Pastor grabbed his Bible and turned to Philippians 4:13, "I can do all things through Christ who strengthens me" *(NKJV)*.

Pastor realized that he would be tested again both in difficulty and in materialistic temptations of the world. He needed the power that only Christ would provide. T needed the strength of Christ to engage his congregation to think, talk, and act more like Jesus as they moved toward a more outreach reality.

T slumped to the side of his desk, placing his elbows on his knees to pray. The prayer was more about changing Joe's heart and asking God to create an opportunity to show this person the excitement of serving rather than being served.

Finishing up the day at the office included some meetings and a baptism in the sanctuary. As he was heading for the office door, the phone rang. Pastor T went back to answer. It was Cole, his Board of Elders chairperson.

"Sorry to bother you so late in the day. I just received three phone calls from people about our missional approach. They're not too happy. It sounded like you may have been contacted by one of them."

"Yes: Joe," T replied. "He sent an email this afternoon. I did call him back, but it didn't go well. He threatened to leave with his money. Cole, how did your conversation go?"

"I got the same threat. How should we handle this situation?"

"First, let's be as understanding as we can with these people. As Pastor, I'm available to talk with them if they desire. However, I believe God wants us to proceed with our missional approach.

"As leaders in Christ's church, I believe we cannot be blackmailed into worldly paradigms with threats involving money and status. It's not like we are leaving our people in despair. I ask you to be considerate of their concerns but steadfast on our destination."

"Oh, I agree with you, Pastor," Cole replied. "I admire your resolve on this issue. Can I tell them to attend our next Elders' meeting to present their concerns?"

"It may not be a good idea to send the message that the Elders are a forum for complaints in the church. I'd like to head it off before it gets that far. Set up a meeting for tomorrow evening from 6:30 to 7:30. Can you and the vice chair attend?"

"I'll check it out with Ed. For sure I'll be there. I'll make some phone calls. Thanks, Pastor!"

Pastor headed for home. He kept thinking about all the good things that were happening, and how it's the one negative thing that gets set on the front burner. As he and Lil were starting their evening meal, Lil asked, "How did things go today?"

"Well, remarks about my efforts ranged from 'remarkable' to 'stupid.'"

"That's nice. Let's start with 'stupid.'"

"It started with 'stupid' and 'nonsense' and got worse from there."

Pastor told his wife about the conversation with Joe. Lil laughed and said, "The guy sounds like a typical S.O.S.!"

"What's that?"

"You have got to be kidding. S.O.S.'s are the ones who are faithful attenders but never want anything to change."

"So what does 'S.O.S.' mean?"

"Same Ol' Stuff!"

T smiled. "I'm glad there's no one listening to this conversation. Sometimes you're too honest."

"That's me! Tell me about the good things that happened today."

Taking a big breath, Pastor said, "There's plenty to tell. Ninety-nine percent of my day was fantastic." Pastor forgot the negative and told Lil about the missional progress.

In his regular quiet time that night, Pastor paged the Bible for reassurance on missional church. As he lifted his favorite mug for a sip of fresh coffee, T again thought about the treasure chest embossed on the cup. It brought to mind the treasures God has given to all believers—and the ultimate promise of eternal life with Him.

T had no problem finding supportive references when he realized the entire Bible was missional and very strategic. He leaned back in his chair and realized he was looking at the trees instead of the forest.

From Genesis through Revelation, God had a plan. He created the plan, executed the plan, and strategically brought people to know and see His plan unfold. His ultimate goal was that all will be told. He handed off the telling part to us, as Christians. He didn't offer a back-up plan. He was relying on us through His family of believers. Pastor was feeling better, and he knew missional had to be the future of Christ's church and he, as pastor, had to empower people into serving within that culture.

LOOKING FOR MEANING:

1. If the church has only one mission of making disciples, shouldn't Christians have a clear vision and purpose for their lives? What is yours?

2. Think about the statement JJ came up with, "serving people." Do you think that is the same as "making disciples"?

3. Why do some people resist change more than others? Would you say Joe was a mature Christian? Why? Why not?

Chapter 14—Use God's Gifts!

"So it is with you. Since you are eager to have spiritual gifts, try to excel in gifts that build up the church."
1 Corinthians 14:12 *(NIV)*

Each gift given to us by the Holy Spirit is to be used for honoring the Lord. These are not natural talents, but supernaturally bestowed to all believers.

Chapter 14 gives us an idea of the array of gifts given to believers to be used for the building up of Christ's church.

Use God's Gifts!

The next day came with Pastor pulling some things together for the meeting with the people who had complained about the shift to missional. He sent a reassuring email to his Elders about the situation, giving them his rationale with supportive Scripture.

The day was filled with meetings and drop-ins. Pastor decided to stay at church until after the 6:30 meeting. He had the conference room set up with a handout of what he wanted to cover.

The Elder chair, Cole, came about 6 p.m. They talked and were united on the approach. The vice-chair arrived in time to be in on most of the discussion. They went into the conference room, and two couples showed up. The man whom Pastor had spoken with the day before didn't appear. Pastor started in prayer and said he wanted to share with them the spiritual reference of this shift to missional. But first, he asked for their individual concerns and their points of view.

Understandably, the two couples were quite nervous as they shared their conversations with Joe, who had called them yesterday. Each couple was influenced by his insistence that all the money was going to support welfare recipients. He painted a picture that was quite an exaggeration. Pastor said that he considered this an opportunity to clarify and calmly consider what

God wanted His people to do. The two couples were very open and wanted to hear Pastor's explanation.

Pastor T gave Biblical references and talk about the Bible being strategic and missional. He explained that "missional" is becoming a disciple who ultimately serves outside the church to create Christian relationships with people who might not know Christ as their Savior. Everything done inside the church is preparation for the mission that Jesus states in the Gospels. T reminded them that serving within the church was important and would continue, but couldn't be considered their primary mission.

The response from the two couples and the Elders was extremely positive. The two couples apologized for their call and said they understood the function of the church better now and would support the Elders' position. They both expressed concern about the damage that the angry man would cause with his misleading statements.

Pastor responded with appreciation and said that their positive attitude would offset the negative. Both parties indicated they'd like to join a young couples group because they didn't know too many people and wanted to grow spiritually. They had been concerned that things like small groups would be discontinued. Pastor told them that small groups were the very thing that would prepare them to go outside the church. As T jotted a note to himself, he told them they would be contacted by someone coordinating small groups.

As a final note, Pastor reassured them that he had no ill feelings toward the man who was upset—and his prayer was that Joe would become open to more involvement in the church.

The couples left and the Elders stayed for another five minutes. Vice chair Ed said with frustration in his voice, "How can information get so screwed up? Pastor, what are you going to do so this doesn't happen again?"

"Ed, this is just part of change," Cole insisted. "You can't blame the pastor for these misunderstandings. In fact, we should be thankful the pastor handled it so discreetly."

"This isn't the last time we will have to manage conflict," warned Pastor T. "We have to remember that most people are understanding and will listen to reason."

"You're both right!" Ed said. "I'm the one overreacting. I just don't like these kinds of phone calls."

All agreed it was a "thumbs-up" meeting. Pastor said he would get an email to all the Elders. As Pastor T finished his writing and organized his desk before leaving, he heard someone in the hallway. Soon Leah and Todd appeared at the door of his office.

"Good to see you folks!" T said affectionately. "What a pleasant surprise. How are you feeling Todd?"

"Oh, I feel great. I suppose you're just leaving for the day?"

"Yes, but I have time for you. What's on your mind?"

"We can come back at a better time if you want. It was kind of a spontaneous thing with us. We saw the light and—"

"Hey, I'd love to talk with you and Leah. Have a seat and tell me what's going on."

"Thanks, Pastor," said Leah. "First, with another week to go, everything is set for the launching at the Village. We could have twenty-five to thirty people drop in from the sounds of the noise around campus. Luke talked to JJ, and he will be there to play his guitar before things get started. We'll get to the point of our being here tonight. Todd, maybe you should explain?"

"Sure! Following the accident, Leah and I talked a lot. We concluded that the thought of losing each other during that process was so powerful, it became evident we're more than just friends. We really mean a lot to each other and find our friendship has led to a loving, more sharing type of intimate relationship. Leah's not ready to jump into a church setting, but we're asking you to counsel us on Christian principles and guide our involvement with each other and God's will for our service to Him."

"Leah," Pastor asked, "how do you feel about this?"

"Exactly how Todd put it. We do love each other; we both want to serve God and to grow together to a deeper relationship based on Christian values. We both respect and admire you and felt we should share this with you. Marriage is probably on the horizon, but not immediately. It's more like a long engagement without a ring."

"Well, I'd be honored. I don't think you're asking about instruction in our denominational doctrine, but you maybe are looking at some premarital counseling and growing in discipleship at the same time. Let me ask if there is anything I should know—like a pregnancy, living together, etc."

"I see you've been down this road before," Todd asserted laughing. "The answer is no. Although we see each other more frequently now, we have our own places and there is no pregnancy to complicate this. Will you do this even if Leah is not a member of our church?"

"Membership should not be a barrier to growing in Christ. Of course I'll do it! In fact, knowing you two, I expect there'll be some pretty tough questions. It'll be good for me to experience and understand your issues. When do you want to start?"

"Evenings would be best for us or even late afternoon," Leah suggested. "Next week will be busy because of the launch, but we want to honor your schedule also."

Pastor looked at his calendar, responding, "How about Thursdays at 4 p.m.? We can go for an hour each session in about a six- or seven-week period of time. Then we can assess where to go from there. It might be that I will suggest a small group for young people in your same situation. The first session can start a week from this Thursday."

"Great," replied Todd. "This means a lot to us. Thanks!"

Pastor was pleased that the day ended on a good note. That evening, he shared the good things with Lil. The days were starting to run together. Although he felt the Village ministry was part of his church responsibility, there would be more people taking shots at him about spending time outside the church. He knew the next few months would require some strategic action on his part for movement of the congregation into his new paradigm.

At the Board of Elders' request, T had already lined up some of his most talented leaders and thinkers to meet that week to brainstorm transformational strategy. It wasn't to be a full strategic planning session—that would come later. However, some of the results would be the basis for a full-blown strategic planning session later in the year before budget time.

The next day, Pastor T headed for church with a cup of coffee in one hand and the wheel of his red pickup in the other. He was expecting about ten to fifteen people for the strategic planning session. He had invited both Liz and Van to facilitate the process.

Pastor was setting up the seating arrangement in a "U" shape so everyone would be facing one another. He selected a room where there would be privacy. Liz showed up with some snacks, and Van brought the soft drinks. Van and Liz got the Smart Board in position and hung some white paper on the wall. Markers were ready to go.

Just like clockwork, fifteen people filed in and took seats at the table. Everyone arrived and was seated before the start time because they knew how Pastor functioned.

"My watch says it is starting time. Let's bow our head for prayer." Following the prayer, T introduced Liz and Van to the group and explained why he had asked them to facilitate the planning discussion. "Liz will get you in the mood. Enjoy your journey."

Displaying the charm and confidence of a seasoned professional, Liz took over. "You have a paper plate with a looped string attached in front of you. There should also be a marker. Please write your first name on the..." Liz explained the protocol to the group.

"Take a look at the Smart Board. There are three empty boxes drawn on the board. By the end of our session the boxes will be filled with your ideas. Before we start, let's go around the room. Introduce yourself and, in one sentence, tell us why you came today."

It set a good tone for the rest of the session. Van took over with his usual organized approach and described the three boxes as Assessment, Clarity, and Strategy.

"Liz is handing out a sheet labeled 'Box ' and titled 'Assessment.' I really hate the word 'Assessment,' so let's just call it, 'As I see it!' You have a list of thirty words on the sheet that could describe mostly anything, but let's apply them to our church. The one rule is, you must be honest. Okay? Cluster yourselves in groups of five, and as your group looks at each word, say to yourself, 'As I see it—this word either describes our church or it doesn't.'"

The three groups of five people had a blast. One group had frequent bursts of laughter and proclaimed themselves the "Fun Group."

"Time's up! Now, as a group, narrow the words you circled down to your final five words that are most descriptive of our church."

Even the "Fun Group" was intensely focused as its members struggled with the task of agreeing on only five descriptive words. Van finished the interaction by recording the aggregate of the impact words in Box 1 on the Smart Board. One word on the board mentioned by every group bothered Pastor T. In his planner he jotted down "Cliquish" and added a comment that was made: "Gossip Groups."

"Are you ready for the plunge into Box 2—Clarity?" Liz forged forward with enthusiasm. "I'd like someone to take a shot at explaining what our vision statement, 'Go...Light the World' means to you."

One participant shouted out, "Fire up every one we make contact with to God's love and saving grace." Another said, "Demonstrate our faith all the time by the way we think, talk, and act." Still another said, "Live our faith in our home, neighborhood, community, and world." A participant, obviously concerned, said,

"Doesn't that start with solid ministries within our church so we're prepared to articulate God's unconditional love for us outside the church?"

Liz didn't miss a beat! Her bubbling personality was reinforcing and encouraging as she summarized the comments into a concise and clear definition of the vision statement.

"How many of you have seen a lighthouse overlooking a large body of water?" Liz asked of the group. Almost all the hands went up. "Great! You know then that the purpose of the enormous light is a fixed destination used by ships to benchmark their location at sea. Likewise, our vision is the beacon—or destination that shines so bright, we keep focused on that.

"The ship's captain, however, still has to have decision-making tools to navigate the ship to that destination. Our tools are called core values. Each of the three values shown on the board must be our conscience as we develop goals, budget, and then manage our ministries."

Liz pointed to each:

-Energized Spiritual Growth

-Ignited Relationships

-Selfless Serving

"Because values represent the best use of energy and resources to get to our vision, they become the stewardship of operational management," Liz concluded. She guided the group through a clarity process for each of the values to set up the strategic process in Box 3, led by Van.

"Thank you, Liz! Now for Box 3—Strategies! In your small group, respond to the question, 'What is the most important effort we should make this coming year in each of the three core values?'"

Using a systematic building-block approach to generate strategies for each core value, Van demonstrated his facilitation skills to involve everyone and bring the group to consensus. The group of fifteen people were engaged and indicated they wanted to continue their involvement.

T met with Liz and Van for a short time after the brainstorming. Van was shaking his head as in disbelief. Liz caught the body language and said, "Van, you look like a light bulb just went on in your head and you can't believe your own thoughts!"

"Something like that! I'm so honored to be asked to partner up with you. You're totally amazing in front of those people."

"You both are amazing," interjected Pastor T. "That's what I wanted to tell you. You got done in two and a half hours what normally takes a full day and then some. I praise God that you accepted my request."

"It was an honor for me," responded Liz. "What you did today, Van, my company pays big money to people who are far less capable than you. I just love your attitude and really enjoy how you take an idea, combine it with another, and present an entirely new perspective."

"I'm hoping that the two of you will take us to the next level when we meet in about three months to start connecting the dots with the ministries that embrace the core values and vision. Can I count on the two of you as a team?"

Liz and Van nodded. Pastor and Van filled Liz in on the ministry progress in the Village. Van was excited about next week's *As We Go* launch. He indicated he'd be there early to meet Dex, Luke, Todd, and Leah. Pastor T informed him that JJ would be doing the pre-event music. Liz said she'd like to hear JJ play and asked if she could drop by with Joey. Pastor and Van extended an invitation to her.

Pastor T excused himself to do some other things and said that he would see them at the launch. That afternoon included some hospital visitations, a Bible study at the nursing home, and a youth group lock-in in the multipurpose room of the church.

As the week went by, Todd and Leah kept T informed about the launch progress. Then, it was finally the day of the launch. Pastor called Lil and told her that he'd be going directly to the Village gathering and not to wait on any dinner that evening.

T arrived at the Village about thirty minutes early. All the young people on the council were busy getting furniture and the food set up. It was no surprise that Van was helping, but Liz and Joey were there also. Liz was helping JJ get his audio system set up while Joey was helping Van pour the M & Ms in bowls. Liz looked so different. Instead of her business attire, she was casual with her hair tied back and wearing jeans and jogging shoes.

"This place looks great," commented Pastor T. "Whose idea was it to put a spot light out front—and where did you get all the balloons?"

"We know how to throw a party," said Leah, bubbling with excitement. "Everything's been donated. JJ even mounted speakers outside. The Village is going to rock tonight."

Dex invited Pastor T to help him unload boxes and display the stuff on the back table for his stained-glass demonstration.

JJ started to play. The music was upbeat and loud. Without a question, JJ was outstanding on the guitar. He was also in control of the crowd. Liz, Leah, and Joey were clapping their hands to the music as the trio danced in the middle of the floor. Even outside, people were moving to the music. They were smiling and having a good time.

Young people started pouring inside as they were directed to the snack table. Some just gathered around JJ and were completely taken over by his music. T tried to get in the background, as did the other two disciples. By this time there were at least forty people inside and another big crowd outside. Somebody had mounted a big flat-screen TV on the wall behind JJ. Todd was perched on a ladder in a corner shooting video, which was shown live on the screen. Even the citywide newspaper was interviewing people and a TV station was shooting footage for the ten o'clock news.

It seemed like it was wall-to-wall people. Acting as the food hosts, Van and Liz were having as much fun as anyone. Joey tagged along and helped work the crowd. They even took food outside to those who were dancing in the streets. T noticed the campus police were walking the streets, giving "thumbs-up" and waving favorably at the young people. T was completely surprised when he saw Phil and five other college-aged people enter the room. T waved Phil over and asked to be introduced to his friends. One was Kyle, who seemed a little reserved about all the attention. T was concerned how Kyle would react if he met Todd. Hopefully, Phil had that covered.

T wondered what would happen when the music stopped. Would they all disappear? Just then, Leah grabbed the microphone and greeted everyone. As JJ tempered the volume, Leah shouted out, "Can JJ play those strings?" Everyone cheered and clapped. She shouted again, "Does God know how to celebrate?" Again, the cheers and clapping.

"This is your lucky night. Jesus loves you and we're going to get to know Him a little better tonight." The crowd inside the building had swelled to more than sixty people. JJ turned the speakers off inside but continued playing so he could be heard outside. Leah introduced Dex, who grabbed the mic and came to the center of the floor.

"God gave me the ability to make beautiful things out of colored glass. I have about ten small pieces floating around the room right now. Take a look and pass them on.

"But first I have to explain about God in my life. A few weeks ago, my friend Luke asked me to get involved in a Christ-centered ministry here in the Village. I told him there was no room for God in my life. Well, he coaxed me to a few of the planning sessions. Bottom line is, I can't say that I am a born-again Christian yet, but I can say that I am proud to be associated with the Christian people who are making this ministry available to us each Wednesday evening for three hours. Their influence is contagious, and I do feel closer to God, but maybe like some of you, I'm here tonight to continue my learning and understanding of Jesus as my Savior." People clapped and cheered.

Dex continued, "I'll only take five minutes and tell you about the art of stained glass. First, I do it because other people enjoy the designs, patterns, light reflection, and the beauty of the finished product." Dex mentioned about six features audience members should inspect as they got a sample in their hands.

Dex concluded, "Next week we will feature a watercolor artist. Her name is Sally. Sally is going to display her art and explain how to get a third dimension in your paintings."

He handed the mic to Leah as she went directly over to JJ and put her hand on his shoulder. She yelled back at the crowd, "Do you like this guy?" The crowd, inside and out, vibrated the rafters with their enthusiasm. "Before JJ packs up his guitar this evening, we've asked him to do one more number. And also a little plug for JJ: next week the space next to us will be the newest business in the Village. So if you have any kind of musical instrument that needs repair, bring it in to the 'Music Maker.'

"I understand this song is one that JJ wrote himself about his life," Leah concluded.

"Thank you, Leah! Yes—and this is the first time I have played it in public. It's dedicated to all the people who brought me from a life on the streets to the privilege of serving God. It's called, 'God Sent Me Angels.'"

People expected an instrumental version. JJ didn't disappoint them as his guitar projected an unforgettable blend of terrific sounds. But JJ also started belting out the words. You could hear a pin drop as the music spoke of despair transformed to hope—of fear transformed to love—Godlessness to Salvation. As he finished his last chord, there was a moment of calmness and silence. Then the crowd went crazy. They loved it! The TV reporters rushed to interview JJ, but all JJ had to say was, 'God Sent Me Angels!'"

"God bless you, JJ," shouted Leah. "I guess JJ will continue to provide some background music during our mixer time. We want to give all of you some time to just hang out, meet people, and enjoy Dex's stained-glass artistry this evening. There are many people who put *As We Go Ministries* together, but I want you to hear from the man himself, Pastor T. We love this dude. Give him a big welcome."

"This is awesome—all of you are awesome," T said, acknowledging the crowd. "As Leah said, God used the talents of a lot of people to bring this opportunity to the Village. It'll continue every Wednesday. We see it as an opportunity to allow God to do His work as Christian relationships are cultivated in each gathering. From these God-filled relationships, God's saving grace will be spread throughout the world.

"Each of you came for different reasons. Some of you are curious, some of you wanted to kick back and enjoy a unique evening, some of you felt drawn to an opportunity to learn more about your Lord and Savior, Jesus Christ. But all of you have a need that is not being met in your heart. Is it possible you can find the answer to that need right here in this spot on Wednesdays in the Village? We feel that through relationships with other people in a Christian setting you will fill that void in your heart with a God who loves you and wants you as part of His family.

"I really encourage you to stay and get involved in the small-group process. You'll not be disappointed! Also, please make it a point to meet someone you didn't know before you came tonight. Will you join me in prayer?"

Pastor T was powerful in his prayer, praising God for bringing everyone together in the name of His Son, Jesus.

"Thank you, Pastor T," Leah said, returning to the mic. "Hey, everybody! I have an assignment for you. Pastor T wants you to meet someone new tonight. Here it is: right now look around and spot someone you don't know, walk over to them and introduce yourself, each of you ask three questions of the other so you know them a little better.

"You're not done yet! The two of you team up with another two people and introduce the person you just met. You'll continue the evening knowing three more people. Come on—don't be shy! I have my eye on somebody," she smiled as she walked across the room and introduced herself to a complete stranger.

The group joined in, and the room was a buzz of talking and laughter. JJ, Van, Dan, and Mick got right into the mix, as did the young organizers. It was a special moment for Liz seeing Joey answering questions about her school and interests.

Keeping an eye on Joey, Liz backed out of the crowd to enjoy the ambience of the evening. She was taken emotionally by what she had experienced so far. It was a fellowship beyond social events to which she was accustomed. There was something genuine about the young people. They were not there to impress, but to just belong. She was also surprised at the staying power of the interaction.

Phil noticed that Todd had walked over to Kyle as part of Leah's get-acquainted assignment. Phil was a little uneasy, realizing neither had any idea the tragedy they had in common. After a few minutes he noticed both Kyle and Todd walking out the door. He wanted to intervene, but he decided to trust that God had things under control.

During the mixer time, four people came up to Dex and asked if he would teach them how to do stained glass. Dex was delighted and set up a class for Tuesdays at 4:00 p.m.

Then, "I'd like to get your attention," pleaded Leah. "Your enthusiasm is wonderful! Pastor T will introduce a Scripture. Then we will follow by splitting into small groups where Luke, Todd, and others will facilitate a discussion of three follow-up questions. This is my favorite part of the evening because the reactions of others in the group always leave something in my mind to ponder during the next week. I find it to be a growing experience in Christ."

Leah noticed that JJ was interpreting what was being said to a couple of guys who were not native English speakers. They were smiling and intent on JJ's Spanish dialogue.

Leah handed the mic to Pastor T. "Pastor T—lead us with your wisdom!" Some of the reporters were still in the crowd, jotting down notes and getting video footage.

"I'm impressed at your openness to love God and love each other. It's my honor to be part of your celebration in the launching of *As We Go Ministries*. I want to make one thing clear to those of you who may feel there is a catch to all this—maybe to attend my church.

"Yes, I'm a pastor at a nearby church, but this is not recruitment for membership. It is, however, an attempt to give you an opportunity right here in the Village to enhance your love for God, to strengthen your love for each other, and to serve God by serving others. The topic tonight is 'Why Me, God?' There are a multitude of dimensions to this question. Why are you sitting here this evening? Why were you given the parents you have? Why do bad things happen to me? Why am I good or poor in science? Why does God love me when I don't deserve His love?

"As we try to answer these questions, most of us start by looking for answers within ourselves. We find blame, pity, excuses, pride, arrogance, defiance, but very little purpose for who and what we are." Out of the corner of his eye he saw Todd and Kyle sitting together. Kyle was nodding his head. "The answer is not in us but in God.

"Colossians 1:16 speaks of purpose in life. This is from the *Message* Bible: 'Everything got started in him and finds its purpose in him. He was there before any of it came into existence and holds it all together right up to this moment.'

"Isn't it amazing that each of us has been designed uniquely by God for a particular purpose? Some of us like to work with our hands like Dex. Some of us have a gift of motivation like Leah. Some of us find our purpose in leadership, others in helping, and still others in teaching. There isn't a person sitting here this evening who wasn't created for a purpose. Maybe some of you have found yours. Some may be placed here tonight to start to recognize their purpose. The point is God has given you the gifts to carry out your purpose in life. Faith and belief in Christ is the beginning of that journey."

Pastor T took exactly five minutes to set the stage for the small- group discussions. The young people were attentive with some taking notes and others just listening.

"My goal tonight is to make you think about the reason for your existence. Let's follow up with discussion. May the Holy Spirit be in your heart and mind as you share with one another. Luke will take it from here."

"Thank you, Pastor. I think each of us has been challenged to think beyond ourselves tonight. We have enough people for about seven tables. Please distribute yourselves using the seven tables available. There will be several of us who will facilitate your group discussion. It's my role as facilitator to keep the discussion on track. It is not to teach or take over the discussion. So everyone get in there and mix it up.

"You were given three questions on the handout. Each question relates to our topic, 'Why Me, God?'"

Everyone quickly grouped themselves around the seven tables. Because of the large number, Luke and Todd requested the disciple leaders to take a table. JJ and Dex wanted to participate and not lead, so Liz and Phil were asked to fill in. Luke explained the time frame for the discussion and encouraged everyone to contribute.

Luke barely got the words out of his mouth and the groups were off and running. Facilitating was about asking questions and keeping the comments on track.

One question was, "Have you ever felt that a certain situation could not be explained and it was evident that it was beyond human reasoning?" It seemed like everyone could relate. One young man said that he had five friends killed tragically in different situations in a short period of time. It was haunting to him because he thought, "Why them and not me?" He said he was so close to them that he could have easily been walking in their shoes at the time of their tragedies. He concluded that God had some kind of a plan for him.

They continued discussing each question, with many contributing to the answers. Luke got everyone's attention and asked if anyone wanted to share their small-group experience with the entire group. Four different people stood up and related how they were inspired by the evening's activities. The fourth person to witness was Kyle.

"Tonight I met the person who was also a victim of an automobile accident that took the life of my brother. The last few months have been filled with self-pity, hate, and despair over my loss. This evening I found a new friendship in Todd and realized that his faith and trust in God helped him heal physically and emotionally from the terrible memory of the fatal accident. I blamed God and anyone else associated with the loss of my brother. Never before had I considered any part of God in my life. Tonight I'm not sure. JJ was also at our table. What an inspiration he is! I hope all of you who haven't found that purpose in your life join me next Wednesday in returning to this gathering. We can help each other get back on track. For sure, I'm coming back."

After the small groups concluded and the visiting died down, everyone involved in planning and organizing the evening stayed for cleanup. Leah and Todd called them together in the middle of the floor. They joined hands, praising God for his presence and blessing the event.

As Pastor T walked in his house that night, Lil yelled out, "Celebrity!" She explained that the TV station was going to use the Village event as a feature on the ten o'clock news.

"Sit down, T, and enjoy the moment. The news is about to come on." The broadcasters hyped the event leading into the news by saying, "Young people and angels right here in the Village coming up at ten."

The two of them relaxed in front of the TV in anticipation of the news coverage. It was time! The camera zoomed in on the news anchor as he began, "Who said young people and angels don't mix?" and then it cut away to JJ singing, "God Sent Me Angels." Random shots followed of the young people clapping and having fun, lights, balloons, and Leah and Pastor T with the microphone. As the focus returned to the news anchor, with JJ's music fading, he said, "Stay tuned for a transformational happening in the Village this evening."

After a series of teasers and breaking for commercial, the coverage of *As We Go Ministries* in the Village was aired. It started with an interview with Pastor T and then cut to the events of the evening. JJ's song was the theme of the feature. The journalist reported Van's generosity in sharing the building, the Disciples Group's involvement, the council, and the purpose of making disciples for Christ. It caught clips of the fun, Dex's show and tell, prayer, sharing in small groups, and even the cleanup and the crew clasping hands in prayer thanking God.

"What great coverage," Pastor humbly acknowledged. "These kids really engaged themselves in making this a successful evening. But the thing that really counts is that each of them witnessed themselves to God as their navigator and strength. I feel like God has been moving all of these happenings to serve Him in a way that we could never do by ourselves."

"You allowed God to transform your ministry, too," contributed Lil. "Remember about a year ago when you were so frustrated and even upset with yourself that you were not able to move the congregation to think missionally. God jumped in and changed all that! You broke away from the status quo ministry. I'm so proud!

"God has a plan here, too!" Pastor wanted the focus on God' work. "It's not just about *our* congregation. It's about God's hand in the ministry that was launched tonight, JJ's marketplace ministry coming up next week, lives of people in small-group interaction, One Punch and his ministry all networking together and the networks launched from dozens of outreach ministries spinning a web that goes on and on. It may have started when God led me to the Village that day and introduced me to a magnificent group of young people to be His ambassadors to spread the Good News of Jesus. It's a good feeling.

"Lil, thank you for your support and understanding. God blessed me with the only woman in the world who could possibly understand me and constantly prop me up to face challenge after challenge."

They hugged each other. It was the thirty-second hug that they had shared almost every day for the past thirty years. The hug tonight was joy and celebration, but other times it was fear, grief, worry, or frustration. Sometimes it meant tears, but it was always the feeling of two people experiencing a sense of oneness and turning it all over to God.

On his way into his study with his favorite mug, T decided to call his brother. It was late, but T didn't want to waste one moment to share how much their relationship meant to him.

LOOKING FOR MEANING:

1. List the different ways the gifts of people were used in this chapter.

2. What was unique about how Pastor T handled the situation with the people upset about the missional approach in the church?

3. Explain how the Village get-together is building up leaders for Christ.

Chapter 15—Strategic!

"Some men arrived carrying a paraplegic on a stretcher. They were looking for a way to get into the house and set him before Jesus. When they couldn't find a way in because of the crowd, they went up on the roof, removed some tiles, and let him down in the middle of everyone, right in front of Jesus. Impressed by their bold belief, he said, 'Friend, I forgive your sins.'"
Luke 5:18–20 *(Message)*

Four friends in a stressful situation, finding they could not get their friend to Jesus by traditional means, become strategic. They lowered him through the roof.

Chapter 15 reveals how God work strategically in our life in ways we would not likely imagine. Pastor T also strategically uses situations to bring people together.

Strategic!

As the sun was coming up, T was already preparing breakfast to surprise Lil. He yelled from the kitchen, "Good morning, Lil! Breakfast is ready to be served in the sunroom."

Lil, walking into the kitchen wearing her robe, yawned, saying, "You're up early T. I thought you'd crash with all the excitement last night.

"I feel great and can't wait for the day to start. Todd and Leah's first counseling session is this afternoon, and the small-group meeting at Oz and Ags is tonight. By the way, are you planning on attending with me?"

"Ags called yesterday, and I told her we'd bring a dessert tonight. She gave me the directions to their home. So, yes! Should I just pick you up at church after your counseling session?" She looked appreciatively at the table, "What a treat this is, T. Thanks!"

After an enjoyable breakfast with Lil, Pastor T headed for church. As he drove into the parking lot he noticed Oz getting out of his car. Pulling up alongside of him, T said, "How you doing, Oz? I didn't think I'd see you until tonight. Is something wrong?" Oz stood outside of T's truck as they talked through the open window. He was noticeably uncomfortable.

"Maybe I totally goofed up," said Oz with some urgency in his voice. "Ags and I know this couple who go to our church that are about our age, and we invited them to our small group tonight. They are a good couple, but he was really upset over what he calls the 'missional shift' in the church. He has apparently talked to you already and expressed his opinion. In his words, he acted like a jerk."

"Yes, I believe I know who you're talking about," replied Pastor. "Is his name Joe? He was quite upset during our conversation. I was hoping he would calm down a bit so he and I could talk."

"Yes, it's Joe. He's calmed down, and he's in big trouble with his wife for spouting off to you. Anyway, they said they'd come to the small group, but that was before I knew about the blow up. Since that time, he and I have talked about JJ and the Boxing for Kids thing. He actually loves that stuff but never knew that's what you meant by missional. He and his wife actually want to get involved with Ags and me helping One Punch. They both saw the Village project on the news last night and were thrilled about reaching out to these young people."

"Oz, you are a missionary! My conversation with Joe has been weighing heavily on my heart. You may have just salvaged another servant for Christ. What can I do to help?"

"Will it be too awkward tonight with them coming? Both he and his wife are embarrassed and called Ags to ask if it was appropriate to come. Especially when they found out that you would probably be there. What should I do?"

"Sounds to me like God put this together. Let's ride it out! My guess is that your friend wants to do the right thing. It may be just the right time to welcome them into your small group. Oz, we are on God's time. My heart tells me that God wants this to happen. If we wait for what we think is the right time, we could really mess it up."

"Really, Pastor? You want them there tonight? I thought I had messed up big time. I'm so relieved. See you tonight!"

Pastor entered the building, where staff and some volunteers were waiting with balloons and spray confetti. It was a celebration over the Village success the previous night. They had punch, cookies, and a cheese platter. The congregational president, Mike, Van, Ed, and Cole were there also. T stayed in the fellowship area and celebrated with them for about twenty minutes. It was a good time to embrace unity on the missional concept.

Sue asked T to say a few words about the Village ministry. He took the opportunity, telling about the impact of these young people who were doing the work of the church. He challenged every person there to begin their missional journey in every ministry in the church, putting the focus on the Great Commission to "Go...Light the world!" Pastor also had a chance to inform Cole, Ed, and Mike about God working through Oz to resolve the miscommunication about missional church. Pastor asked Phil to comment about Kyle. It was quite emotional for Phil, because it was the first breakthrough in Kyle's negative attitude about God. Phil ended with, "I saw firsthand what a missional heart," referring to Todd, "combined with God's power can do."

As with most days in a pastor's life, this one was busy. However, it was also different. To Pastor T, it was like the first day of the rest of his life. During his quiet time, T opened his Bible to a familiar Scripture, Philippians 3:14: "I press toward the goal for the prize of the upward call of God in Christ Jesus" (NKJV).

These words of the Apostle Paul had always inspired T, but at this moment in his life it was like the words came alive. Pastor T walked over to the white board hanging on his office wall and wrote in the upper corner, "Run the race!" He drew a smiling face at the end of the statement. As he stepped back and looked at the words, so many things came to mind. He visualized urgency, focus, energy, strength, preparation, persistence all wrapped up in Jesus' command: make disciples!

After a full day of meetings and administrative stuff, Pastor looked forward to his counseling session with Todd and Leah.

The couple showed up right on time. Todd said, "Good afternoon, Pastor! Are you ready for us?"

"Not only ready, but looking forward to the privilege of growing together."

"Come on, Pastor," remarked Leah. "This is a slam dunk for you."

"When we mix people and God, nothing's a slam dunk. What I meant was that God has great plans for each of you, and I'm thrilled to be part of that journey. Have a seat and we'll get started."

Pastor walked over and closed the door. He had the couple sit together in a love seat and he intentionally seated himself in a chair adjacent to them with a coffee table in front of them. Pastor had found that sitting behind his desk was a barrier.

"Wasn't that a blast last night in the Village?" Todd said. "I'm still pinching myself—it doesn't seem real."

"Todd and Leah, your team did a magnificent job putting that together. Everything was remarkable, but the interaction that took place in the small groups openly talking about Jesus was thrilling. Todd, I can't thank you enough about taking Kyle under your wing."

"Yeah. I think that was set up by God himself. It was one of those circumstances that just flowed, and the results were all good. He did ask if I could come to one of the meetings Phil is having with him and his friends. I told him I'd be honored. Pastor, I believe the Village effort is going to open doors that we can't even comprehend."

"I agree!" commented Leah. "But, Pastor, what does 'Run the race!' mean on the white board?"

"Thank you for noticing. I just wrote that on the board today. It represents my commitment of Philippians 3:14."

Pastor used it as an introduction to the counseling session by relating the meaning of the Scripture and how we must run the race with our optimum ability and focus.

"I brought my bottled water," Leah said, pointing to the table. "Do you mind, Pastor?"

"Not at all! I'd like to cover two things in our first session. First, let's pray." The three of them clasped hands as Pastor led them in prayer.

"I'd like to encourage you to share your visions for the future and how they involve each other. Later, I'd like to introduce the myth of a 50/50 relationship. Todd, maybe you can start by explaining how you see your future with Leah."

"We've talked quite a bit about this. At this time each of us is still pursuing our own interests and we have not really settled in on any kind of routine in our lives. The one thing we have in common besides being attracted to each other is our passion for Christ in our lives. Right now we continue to serve God in various capacities, but we realize that we both must grow continuously in our knowledge and understanding of God's Word also. We have some common interests, like physical fitness, sports, learning, and travel."

Pastor looked Leah, asking, "How about you, Leah?"

"The answer to this question is still developing, but Todd expressed my feelings, too. The one thing I can add is our personalities. We both like to be around and deal with people. I am probably the more outgoing, but Todd is the person others lean on and seek out because of his concern for people's issues. I am the organizer, where Todd can discern what people have in their hearts. He is also a visionary in that he sees a bigger picture. He likes to turn the bigger picture over to me to identify the pieces and make it complete. God's important to us. Right now the gap in our lives is that I see most churches as restrictive, with a kind of club mentality. People are so busy keeping the church going, there's no time to do what church is really all about."

"How's this gap affecting your relationship?" T asked. "Todd, do you see Leah's perception of the church as a concern in your relationship?"

"No, I've never perceived it as a deal breaker in our relationship, if that's what you mean, but it's often part of our conversation. My position is that church forms the foundation for receiving God's Word and, of course, the Sacraments. Actually, Leah agrees. It's the logical place for us to grow spiritually so we can be more effective in our service to God."

Leah followed up on Todd's statement. "Today's church doesn't think, talk, or act like I do. I don't want to spend time discussing who is going to dish up the hot dish so the church members can eat or how it has always been done a certain way. I always tell Todd that he grew up with it, so it is part of his DNA. At the same time, he admits to not being captivated by the status quo attitude within the church. All I can say is that we're on that journey to clarify our feelings so it doesn't affect our relationship. It's not about God's teachings, but the church has become stiff, redundant, and self-serving. I just don't think Jesus would be comfortable with that."

"We didn't know it would be part of our relationship building, but it's significant," Todd interjected. "Pastor, you're probably the only one we know who might understand how we're thinking. We see ourselves as Christians! We believe in the Trinity, the redemption that Jesus Christ gives us, God's creation; and we profess our faith openly. We need the church in order to grow spiritually but also the freedom to feed our passion of ministering to those who are not spiritually healthy."

"It didn't take long for this discussion to get challenging," asserted Pastor T. "For what it is worth, many in the church would agree with your observations. Our church is experiencing a transformation that will address exactly what you're talking about. It just doesn't happen overnight. People like the two of you can help with this transformation. However, for now, let's stick to your relationship. I promise we'll come back to this discussion.

"Have you heard that every relationship should be a 50/50 situation, Todd?"

"I think you might be talking about the idea that each person in a relationship must contribute 50 percent or match the effort of the other."

"That's good! I'm about to tell you that it doesn't work." Todd and Leah seemed startled by T's bold statement. "I want to build a case for 100 percent effort. You see, if one person in this relationship gives something less than 100 percent, what happens, Leah?"

"The other person feels that they no longer have to give 100 percent."

"I get it!" Todd continued confidently, "Each person thinks that they only have to match the effort of the other person but not any more than that. The result is less and less effort. More and more arguments, and the relationship is in trouble."

"Right on! What happens if one person stays at 100 percent and doesn't play the equalization game?"

"It sets the standard for the one giving less," Leah contributed. "We know that most people in a relationship will strive to meet the effort made by the other as long as it is a reasonable expectation."

"Right again! How difficult will it be for either of you to remain at 100 percent?"

Leah, feeling she knew the answer, offered, "Well, I'd see it as a real challenge because our emotions are involved. If Todd wouldn't help me with clean up after a meal, I might start ragging on him about making his own meals. And so it goes!"

Less confident, Todd said, "I've never thought of this before, but this could easily be a deal breaker in a relationship. It's a matter of attitude. I know sometimes I'm disappointed in how someone may treat me. My first reaction is to treat them the same way. God's way would be to rise above that and continue to treat the other person in a respectful manner."

"Great!" Pastor had them on track. "Relationship is one of the most valuable things we have. If the relationship is struggling, it has an impact on everything else we do. What I'm saying is, it's worth 100 percent effort all the time. It's true even if the other party gives less. At that point we have a choice—we can either feel sorry for ourselves and give less or decide to do the right thing by maintaining our 100 percent."

Leah suggested, "I'd guess that giving 100 percent at first is a real effort, but eventually it becomes a way of life."

"That would be ideal," Pastor noted, "but what I've seen is that we tend to get a little sloppy about our relationships and then realize the 100 percent has slipped. At that point we scramble to get it back on track. In most cases, the relationship requires good communications and constant adjustment for both parties."

Todd asked, "What happens when one person in the relationship consistently gives 100 percent and the other never rises to the occasion and instead begins to take advantage of their partner's commitment to 100 percent?"

"Excellent question, Todd! That's a problem. No one should ever be a doormat because of their forgiving behavior. If the couple can't work it out, they may need a third party, such as a Christian counselor, involved. We're not perfect, and sometimes it doesn't work out. However, if this 100 percent rule were followed by married couples, our divorce rate would not be at 50 percent!"

"Good answer, Pastor. Leah and I have plenty to talk about. I'm glad we're doing this each week. Pastor, I think our hour's up, and we know you have another commitment."

"You're right. This has been an awesome session. Let's close in prayer."

Pastor asked Todd to pray. Afterward, Leah and Todd left looking forward to the next week's session. T rushed out to the parking lot, where he saw the Silver Streak and Lil waiting. He hopped into the car, and Lil already had the GPS set to take them to Oz and Ag's house across town.

As they arrived, Liz was just opening her car door as JJ climbed out the passenger side.

Getting out of the Silver Streak, Lil yelled, "Liz, I see you have a passenger tonight."

"Yes, I told JJ I'd pick him up at the Village. It was just too far on his bicycle."

"Greetings, JJ," said Pastor T warmly. "Riding in that Mercedes is a long way from the streets."

"You're right! I see you drove in class tonight too, with the General chauffeuring you."

"His casting arm is bad," responded Lil. "I have to keep him in shape for the big catch like you, JJ."

Oz was at the door to welcome them into his home. They were led into a good-sized family room that Oz and Ags had built onto the back of the house. Ags made the introductions to the new guests, Dee and Joe. Everyone was invited over to a snack bar to take some food and a beverage.

When they were seated, Oz again welcomed everyone and said that he'd like to start with prayer. Oz had given this prayer some thought, because he prayed that God would use this small group, with all of its human imperfections, to make a positive impact on the world. Oz then turned it over to Pastor.

"Oz and I discussed the format of this evening, and I brought enough Participant Guides for everyone. It is a DVD-based small-group Bible study that's six weeks long and includes individual devotions for us to read between sessions, questions that will guide the discussion, and a teaching video. It's my experience that every group needs some structure to make sure there's a good mix of social interaction and spiritual growth.

"This study starts with an icebreaker. On page three of your book, it asks us all to respond to the statement, 'In my faith journey, I often find that I...' Each of us is to complete the statement with our own experience."

"I'll start!" Oz volunteered. "In my faith journey, I often find that I get derailed between weekends." He went on to explain what he meant.

Tom stepped up and said, "Oz, I relate to what you just said. In my faith journey, I often find I don't commit to a regular time to study the Bible and meditate on the meaning. A lot of it has to do with my erratic schedule at the hospital."

"In my faith journey," asserted Liz, "I often find I don't surrender myself to God's plan. Lately, I've found out that I can't fix some family things and I've become better at turning it over to God."

Everyone volunteered except the new guests and Pastor T. Pastor thought it might be good for him to say something to see if he could get Joe and Dee to talk.

"In my faith journey, I often find that I fail miserably at considering other people's feelings. Although I try to communicate effectively, I allow myself to sometimes move forward before all the bases are covered, forgetting that someone might have a different perspective."

Hitting Joe on the shoulder, Dee said, "Your turn, Joe!" Joe looked like he wanted to run out of the room. Dee continued, "Joe, if you want to get off my 'You're in trouble list…'"

"Yes, dear!" Looking down at his folded hands, Joe began, "What Dee is talking about is an email I sent in a rage to Pastor T about how stupid I thought this missional emphasis was at church. Pastor was kind enough to call me so we could talk about it, and I blew him off and acted like a jerk. It all happened because I thought I knew something, but I didn't have a clue. I didn't realize what 'missional' was until we got to talking with our friends, Oz and Ags. The embarrassing thing is I liked the concept after I understood it.

"So, in my faith journey, I often shoot myself in the foot by spouting off without good information. It certainly is not what Jesus would do, and the bonus is, it gives people permission to dislike me." Directing his attention to T, Joe apologized, "Pastor, I'm sorry. I'll understand if you don't want me involved."

Pastor T walked across the room toward Joe and held out both fists. Joe butted them with his own as the rest clapped. Pastor said, "Oz mentioned that we are an imperfect group of people who are gathered so we can learn more about our God and also allow Him to use us for service to Him and His people.

"Joe, you don't have to feel you are the only person who ever took a few shots at me. Actually, I realized from your reaction that I have to do a better job at explaining and defining missional. Thanks for bringing it to my attention." Everyone laughed again. Joe seemed relieved as his wife gave him a hug.

Dee finished up by completing her faith statement. Oz loaded the DVD in his player and used the remote to activate session one, titled, "Use It or Lose It!" They all watched and jotted down some of the "fill-in the blanks" in the guide. Following the eight-minute teaching video, T reviewed the fill-ins and went right to the questions in the discussion guide. The topic was about spiritual gifts the Holy Spirit distributed to every Christian to be used to build up the kingdom of God.

The last question was, "What are you going to do about it?" Members of the group couldn't wait to respond and Pastor got a few surprises.

After hearing JJ's story at Pastor T and Lil's house, Vi recalled, "Everyone wanted to do something. We made some assignments to each person, and we are going to get our reports tonight.

"Tom and I were responsible to get information from the hospital. We met with the hospital administrator to see if there was any way we could identify inner-city programs that attract and help young people stay out of trouble or work with rehabilitation to help young people get off the streets. When we arrived for our meeting, the administrator had three other people in the conference room that are currently involved with inner-city services.

"When we mentioned the Boxing for Kids program, they all indicated that was a 'thumbs-up' program. They referred to One Punch as Father Paul. His professional fight name was One Punch. We were told that there were only a few places like Father Paul's gym. They were all in need of resources.

"We found out that kids very seldom make it off the streets unless they work with one of these professionals to make contacts in better neighborhoods. They normally will stay in gangs to survive instead of trying to improve themselves. JJ, can you comment?"

Nodding his head, JJ added, "On the streets these places you're referring to were called Angel Shelters—or that's what I called them. The difference between the dozens of ordinary shelters and these is the person in charge, like One Punch. You're expected to do chores and get involved in the program. The others are just a place to sleep with your eyes open.

"There are two more ways to survive. One is to join a gang and take shelter with them. You can usually trust gangs if you're accepted, but you're expected to prove yourself all the time by doing some really nasty things. The other way was my way—travel with someone you trust and find a vacant building, sewer, park, bridge, etc. and mind your own business.

"The best chance for street kids is the Angel Shelters. The head dude, like One Punch, has contacts. The trouble is most kids don't make it because they don't fit. They can't read or write. They talk like I do, and they only have street math."

"JJ just confirmed what we learned," Tom remarked. "Many of these kids need some basic academic skills and in some cases English as a Second Language. The best place for them to receive any motivation for some basic training is at these primary places where they trust the coordinator. There's a need for some kind of transition to schools or someplace they can start to experience a transformation to a life with some hope.

"We did talk about the hospital staff volunteering for some preventative medical attention at Father Paul's gym. Maybe we can prevent some infections, pneumonia, and diseases."

Oz leaned forward with his comments. "Ags and I were assigned to find out more about the Boxing for Kids Gym program. We made contact with One Punch, and he invited us to tour his building. In the meantime, we were visiting with Joe and Dee, and we invited them to go with us. There's safety in numbers! We had a great tour and visit. It's a fairly large building that I guess is city owned. Father Paul has a full boxing gym set up with all types of training stations. We were surprised that he lives right there and has other sleeping rooms for homeless kids. He told us they're full most of the time. The place has a kitchen, but the kids usually have to go to a make-shift soup kitchen on the same block for one meal a day."

"These kids have nothing except the friendship of One Punch and the self-esteem he gives them," Ags added. "It makes me sad knowing what their chances are to be happy. Joe or Dee, do you want to add anything?"

Joe surprised everyone with his passion. "My heart goes out to those kids. If that's missional, I'm all in! The real void seems to go back to what Tom was saying—a good transition where kids are not thrown to the wolves and set up for failure."

"I did talk to One Punch after your visit," commented JJ. "Man, he is encouraged by your interest and has some ideas. We worked out a mentoring thing. He has one kid that he feels should move on. I'm going to take him on as an experiment. Hey—I thought I was the experiment," he smiled humbly.

"He can bunk in my apartment until we find something better. His first language is Spanish, and he can pick up a little more English from me. He and a friend attended the Village launch with me. He plays a guitar, so he'll work with me at the shop. He knows I won't be able to pay him, but he'll get a place to stay and meals. One Punch and Luke are going to talk to someone about spending some time at the Village to teach this kid how to read.

"Man, I'll teach him how to cook, too!" JJ laughed, "Or maybe he can teach me how to cook. That's one of the goals that One Punch talked about. These kids don't usually have independent living skills, and they have never had to pick up after themselves."

"I had the fun assignment," Liz said enthusiastically. "Vi asked me to get familiar with the Village project and see if there is any potential connection to the Boxing for Kids program. Pastor T and Van gave me an invite to the opening night, so I got to see it firsthand.

"We have already heard tonight that there can be a viable connection to One Punch and his kids. From what I saw, we can network a number of services together. I think we must maintain a Christ-centered focus. What I experienced last night was completely inspirational. My daughter and I talked for an hour about how we felt and how God is opening our hearts.

"If we allow God to work in the hearts of these young people who are attending every Wednesday, we can create a ministry base to help inner-city kids in the future. My company can throw in some resources, too, and it can become an opportunity for these young people to serve as mentors like JJ just explained. Allowing God to work inside us and lead us over the next few weeks might be the best action we can take."

"I agree!" exclaimed Dee. "If we do too much too fast we might miss real opportunity and burn ourselves out at the same time. In the meantime, there are some things we can do to help One Punch. His building's in need of some maintenance. Even the kitchen could be updated and some of the sleeping rooms painted."

Having been totally unaware of these events, Pastor T responded, "I had no idea God was working in all of you like this. It sounds like our strategy should be to give JJ any support we can as he mentors the first street person. JJ, would you be willing to keep in touch with Liz and Van about the needs of this young man? I will also help in any way I can."

"You guys are awesome!" JJ exclaimed. "I'm doing the easy stuff!"

"Tom and Vi, you have connections in the area schools. Will you contact them to see what services might be available for JJ to help this young person and at the same time coordinate with Luke?" Pastor suggested.

Honored that she was asked, Vi responded, "Absolutely!"

Oz offered, "Maybe Ags, Dee, Joe, and I can make another visit to One Punch and make a list of Saturday maintenance projects. We can coordinate the supplies and set up a time on Saturdays for all of us to hop in our work clothes and get some things done at the gym."

Responding to Oz's suggestion, T continued, "Oz, if you will take leadership of the maintenance as a short-term project, there may also be another small group in the church that will help on Saturdays. I also know our youth are looking for serving projects. I'll get them in touch with you."

"We're really on a roll," Dee offered. "Joe and I have some connections with a wholesale grocery supplier. They give food at certain times of the week to pick up. Maybe we can keep JJ's kitchen and the gym kitchen partially stocked."

"What a productive evening!" T concluded. "If I can use your words, JJ, 'We're rockin' n' rollin'. I'm totally impressed with you people. Considering the diversity of your group, you have come together with all of your skills and contacts to serve God's people. Seeing God's handiwork warms my heart.

"There might be times when Lil and I will not be able to attend the small group, but you have plenty of leadership. Remember to maintain the blend of fellowship, growing in Christ, and serving by using the curriculum.

"Let's stand and pray." Everyone clasped the hand of the person next to them. "Would anyone like to begin?"

"I would!" announced Joe. "Dear God, I've a lot on my mind, and I have to say this now or I may not have courage later. My words may not be adequate for You, but I think You are listening. I feel like such a failure—the way I behaved with Pastor T and jumping to conclusions when I wasn't clear about his intentions.

Also, these people tonight should have kicked me out for my actions, but they didn't. They invited me in! Right now I feel so useful. Help me to overcome sticking my foot in my mouth. Help these people to hold me accountable. God, I'm so thankful You placed me here this evening to be able to use what You gave me to honor You by serving others."

The individual prayers continued. JJ, in his humble manner, brought everyone together as he not only thanked God but challenged God to take his life and make it useful. He said, "God, You have placed me in the middle of Your plan. I don't understand it. I don't know what You want. I don't even know if I can do it. I do know that You are my King. Just like the King who watched my back on the streets, You're my heavenly King. I trust You! I love You!"

After the prayer, Ags served dessert. No one was ready to leave. The excitement over a ministry that was unfolding brought them closer together and made them respectful of each other's gifts. Liz asked JJ to play his guitar and lead them in a song. Closer relationships prevailed, and it ended as a fulfilling evening.

On the way back to church to get the truck, Lil commented about the perfect evening. Pastor responded, "You're right, Lil; everything really clicked tonight, but did you watch JJ? He led tonight with humor, humbleness, encouragement, action, and confidence. All the time he never took credit but gave the glory to God. God's Spirit is working overtime. I feel so blessed that God gave us JJ to link us all together."

"Now that I think about it, you're right," recalled Lil. "JJ's leadership style is unique and kind of sneaks up on you. T, here's your truck. See you at home."

LOOKING FOR MEANING:

1. What do you think about the 50/50 relationship myth that Pastor discussed with Leah and Todd?

2. Have you ever put your foot in your mouth before you took the time to know what the other person meant? Describe what you thought was compelling about Joe at the small-group meeting.

3. Can you identify the person(s) who demonstrated the following spiritual gifts as they planned their servanthood happenings?

Leadership

Administration

Discernment

Serving

Faith

Giving

Encouragement

Chapter 16—Interactive Process!

"...I have voluntarily become a servant to any and all in order to reach a wide range of people: religious, nonreligious, meticulous moralists, loose-living immoralists, the defeated, the demoralized—whoever. I didn't take on their way of life. I kept my bearings in Christ—but I entered their world and tried to experience things from their point of view. I've become just about every sort of servant there is in my attempts to lead those I meet into a God-saved life..."
1 Corinthians 9:19–23 *(Message)*

Finding common ground with other people requires one to be interactive. When you are interactive with the Great Commission in mind, it becomes a process you repeat daily.

Chapter 16 reflects on the interactive process that was necessary to grow a missional ministry with multiple dimensions.

Interactive Process!
Five Years Later

Five years after launching the Village gathering, the original members of the *As We Go Ministries* Council sponsored an anniversary celebration. You know—any reason for a party! Leah was the creativity behind a full day of activities in the Village. As you can imagine, it was big, with a parade, a ministry fair, music, dancing, witnessing from many segments of the community, carnival, arts/crafts, and indoor and outdoor worship opportunities.

The city mayor even spoke about *As We Go Ministries'* impact: reduced gang activity, a lower inner-city crime rate, and higher literacy transition of homeless people. The *As We Go* Council honored JJ and Van for their entrepreneurial ministry efforts and celebrated Todd and Luke's entrance into the office of the ministry. Approximately two thousand people attended, with great support from T and Lil's church.

Pastor T's brother, Tim, attended the celebration with his wife, Gwen. In spite of his confinement to a wheelchair, Pastor

Tim took an active part in the festivities and really connected with JJ. Gwen, a teacher, was amazed at the diversity of believers who had committed themselves to missional serving.

The results of the previous five years confirmed to T that his calling to be more missional was truly God's will. His brother added to T's joy by showing up unexpectedly to support him on this special day.

Tim and his wife were on a mission to meet all the people his brother had talked about the previous five years. They had a good visit with Van and Liz and found out about their wedding plans and the excitement of having JJ as Van's best man.

After learning that Todd was three months from finishing his seminary course work, Tim shared stories about preparing oneself for pastoral ministry. Todd and Leah were excited to tell the couple about Pastor T's influence, which led to their being married by T in a Christian church ceremony. Leah explained that her heart for Jesus led her to switch career goals. She had earned her degree in Special Ministry, giving her a choice of several areas in which she could serve in a called capacity.

The visiting couple met members of the original small group and heard about the phenomenal growth of small groups in the church and the community. They also had the pleasure to meet every member of the original Disciples Group and also Cole, who had become a community ministry leader, helping businesses function as marketplace ministries.

Other conversations with staff, church ministry leaders, and Village folks who were in different stages of their spiritual growth inspired Tim and Gwen to think of ways they could advance the missional agenda where God had placed them.

It was mid-afternoon when T spotted JJ walking alongside Tim's wheelchair and heading up the hill to the park. T nudged Lil and said, "I know Tim and Gwen will be leaving soon. Let's spend some time with them."

"Good idea," responded Lil. "Gwen and I'll pick up a pizza and some soda at the food tent. We'll meet you at the park in a few minutes."

Tim and JJ had made themselves comfortable near a table by the time T caught up. JJ asked, "Should I leave so the two of you can hang out?"

"JJ, you're part of this family. Please stay," requested T. "I want my brother to know you as family also. The General will be joining us after she and Gwen pick up a pizza."

"Man, you guys are too awesome," JJ said. "I haven't eaten all day—bring it on: I'm always hungry."

Tim inquired, "I have many questions. So, JJ, what was it that finally led you to Christ?"

"Oh, after I realized that your brother really cared about me and didn't have a con, I started listening to what he was saying about Jesus. Man, I think about all the grief I caused him, not understanding he was God's messenger. When I finally felt God's love, I surrendered. Pastor Dude called that 'born again'."

"God is great. Bless you, JJ. Say, let me ask you a question 'Thaddaeus,'" Tim responded with a mischievous grin on his face.

T interrupted with, "Don't go there, brother. JJ knows my secret, and he doesn't need any devious encouragement."

The three of them laughed. Then Tim became serious, "I got a good look at all the kingdom-building in the Village, but T, were you able to see significant missional change in your church?"

Laughing, T said, "Sometimes it seemed that God led us right through the wall. I experienced many scars and bruises. We lost three families because they didn't feel comfortable with the missional vision. They were our friends also. Even doing the right thing is sometimes heartbreaking. But the flip side of that is each family still stays in touch with us, and they seem to be happy serving God in a different church.

"The good news is the many people who now live their faith every day in their community. Others have grown beyond local ministry effort to short-term mission opportunities throughout the world. Some have committed themselves to full-time mission work in other countries. Tim, that's significant because the number before was almost zero. Also, through God's direction, we're now a primary source of young people going into the office of the ministry and church-related vocations. We learned some things, too. Our previous notion that membership in the church was a valid measurement of success was country club thinking. Actually, we've moved beyond attendance to counting those who meet the criteria of growing spiritually."

"How about Bible study?" asked Tim.

"Our Bible study participation has increased proportionately. I'm not just talking numbers but real interaction and challenging questions as a measurement indicator, too. In addition, our small-group emphasis increased ten-fold. Without small groups, we'd never have had the phenomenal response to serve outside the church."

"Y'all impress me," inserted JJ. "I still haven't been in your church, but you involved me, kicking and screaming, in some front-line stuff."

"You were the key to making it all happen," said Pastor T. "JJ, don't you realize your influence on all the missional progress in the last five years?"

"It ain't got anything to do with me. There I go again with bad English. Liz would rattle my cage."

Listening and enjoying JJ's references, Tim asked, "JJ, why do you play down your effectiveness? You're a smart person, and you certainly realize the extensive role you played in that missional effort."

"Man—you know—I will never be totally smart. I've learned a lot, but I've got a long way to go. I honestly don't see my participation as anything that I should brag about. You see, through my eyes, I have been God's instrument to do what I do best—that's love and serve others. If I have been an influence, then I should give glory to God."

"Wow," Tim responded, "I'm impressed. Most church workers don't have insight with that much depth. Good answer, JJ."

Entering the edge of the park, Lil shouted, "Hey, food's ready. Anybody hungry?"

JJ rushed to help by carrying the beverage cooler. On the way to the table, Lil kept trying to get JJ to talk about the recognition he had received at the morning ceremony. JJ was obviously flattered, but he checked his emotions and remained humble about all the attention.

Finally, they were all seated. JJ motioned with his hand that he wanted their attention. "Hey, will you guys let me pray?" Recognizing JJ's request as heartfelt, Pastor T responded, "JJ, you're always welcome to pray at our table."

Clasping T and Lil's hands, JJ glanced back and forth into their eyes, saying, "Guys—I'm the luckiest street kid ever! God placed you in my life. Man, just sitting here at your table is like sharing heaven with God. Like—you never let me down—always had my back." Squeezing their hands, he concluded, "Um—I just want to say thank you!" Tim and Gwen joined in the prayer circle and acknowledged the deep sense of appreciation JJ was displaying.

Bowing his head, JJ praised God for being in his life, thanked Him for the people who lift him up every day and for the food and generous hearts of Pastor T and Lil. As he finished, he wiped a tear, and said, "Sorry, it's like you're a part of me." Clearing his throat, he continued, "Man, it smells good. Let's devour that pizza!"

Motioning for JJ to take the first piece, Lil said, "Just so you know, you're embedded in our hearts forever. We love you so much." Then she gave him a big hug.

Continuing the discussion that Tim had started, JJ said, "Hey, General, you and the Pastor put a blast of energy into your church and *As We Go Ministries*. There must have been times when it was really tough."

Lil responded, "I remember the struggles, challenges, and blessings that come along with transforming our congregation—and God transforming T to a missional pastor. It was tough, but God blessed us with guidance, courage, and the right resources."

"Pastor Dude, you told me your experience was tough on your ego and that you had failures. What did you mean?"

T smiled. "First, I learned that God must come first. Also, people want it simple and not the terminology baggage we carried with us from seminary. Second, I had to build up leaders—it takes more than one to shepherd the flock. I admit that was a little threatening for me. Third, as a spiritual leader, I had to step out front with the vision. And, of course, I failed miserably—with my own staff! It was my fault that we had silos, turf battles, and entitlement games in the church," T admitted. "My leadership was based on what I thought empowerment was all about—give them the ball and let them go! Well, I was wrong."

"Sounds like I've heard that before," recalled Tim. "Brother, you're too tough on yourself," he admonished, adding, "It's so rewarding to see God's handiwork in the growth of *As We Go Ministries*. I think someone said today that there are over six hundred people growing in Christ—and it's still growing!"

"Hey, brother," JJ said with an admiring smile, "you're short on your numbers. If you include all the relationships in Transformation—we're at thousands. Man, Tom took us all on a ride when he caught fire—it led to 'Transformation.'"

"You're correct, JJ," Pastor T noted. "It's not just the Village and college people—God's light has been spread all over the city. Tom started the 'Give kids hope!' process. He got the entire small group busy connecting agencies, schools, medical services, shelters, etc., to build a process that tied all these together to give kids hope. That process is now called 'Transformation.' People like One Punch start the process by recommending a young person who is ready. The referral comes to Vi, who has an office in the *As We Go Ministries* building. She and her volunteers customize a combination of services that will most benefit that young person."

Gwen asked, "JJ, how do you fit into that picture?"

"Hey," 2J's face lit up as he explained, "that's where my 'Transitional Mentoring Academy' enters the scene. One Punch works with me also. These kids are a little older and usually have other problems."

"JJ, my brother has told me that you've built a network of five other people like yourself to help these young street people." Tim continued, "I also understand your business is doing great. Tell us about it."

"Yeah, I have five of my street brothers helping me. They are great at relating to the needs of these kids and mentoring them to improve their skill sets and success in a world they don't know about.

"The Music Maker is turnin' money, but the cool thing is the ministry that happens in my man cave. Pastor Dude tells me that the Music Maker is the perfect example of a marketplace ministry. I have tried to stick to my goal of serving people. Like I said, it's not the money. It's relationship building. The guys I mentor experienced the same thing I did. People want to talk about Jesus and all we have to do is remove the barriers.

Gwen asked, "What's the main thing that helped you make the transition from street kid to Christian ministry leader?"

"Things don't impress me much," answered JJ, "but that Bible the General gave me five years ago is my treasure. I wore it out. You know, I've penciled notes on every page and a few pages are even loose. Right now I'm using a couple other Bibles. I don't miss a night of study. But the original Bible sits on the counter of the cave. People are so curious. They ask me if I really read what's in it. I just open it and flip the pages to show them all my notes. That Bible has started many conversations about Jesus. Gwen, I guess that's the main thing." Turning to T, JJ asked, "Pastor Dude, was it your plan all the time to have another church in the Village?"

"No, JJ: that was God's plan. Every pastor dreams about planting a church—it's part of our DNA to build God's kingdom.

However, in all honesty, I never saw that coming. It just shows that God's plan and His timing is something we don't know until it smacks us in the face. In this case, He used all of you in the Village, our Disciples, and our congregation to start a twenty-first-century church right in the Village.

"Tim and Gwen probably don't know your financial generosity. Van told me you've sent a check to the church for 15 percent of your profits every month for five years. And, you're too modest to tell about the financial help you give those you mentor."

"Come on, Pastor Dude, you're embarrassing me." JJ diverted the conversation, "Tell your bro about the people coming to the Village church."

"Well, Tim and Gwen, I'm pleased to say we have young people coming from all over the city to attend the church in Van's building. Ninety percent of these people were not affiliated with a church before. It's the spirit of feeling compelled to serve that is the dominant feature in *As We Go Ministries* and that carried over into the Village church. Missional attitudes have made giving a privilege, resulting in almost everything going to serve other people. Serving ourselves isn't even a consideration."

JJ remarked about Leah's commitment to keep the church missional. "Leah's the nuke of the Village church."

"By 'nuke,' do you mean nucleus?" asked Pastor T. JJ nodded, and T agreed, "Yes, and she never runs out of energy."

"How did you come up with the name of the Village church?" Gwen inquired.

T explained, "Liz and Leah came up with the name 'Second-Effort Gathering.' Liz started it by saying, 'We express our faith in many forums to honor God—usually because our first effort, without God, failed us.' Leah yelled out, 'Second-Effort Church.' Liz responded, 'I'm surprised at you, Leah. I thought church wasn't your shelter.' Then Leah said, 'You're right! How about 'Second-Effort Gathering'?'"

"Right on!" JJ remembered, "I was there when Liz and Leah were sparring. I think Leah still resists what she perceives as the traditional church. Of course, I do, too! Todd and Leah launched the 'Serve Groups.' Dude, they even make you look good at weekend worship."

"You're right! They team up to help me with the worship services. Leah has also taken ownership of the youth. She has claim to a success formula for youth: [(Relationships + Service x Growth) = Exponential Discipleship]."

"On our tour today, I noticed the formula painted on the wall of the youth room," said Gwen. "I think that's quite profound."

"Hey, Dex painted that on the wall of the Youth Hide Away," announced JJ. "Man, he could be a graffiti artist. He's good!"

"Yes, he is," Pastor agreed. "Second-Effort Gathering is described by Leah as giving glory to God with a blend of informality and simplicity. She says, 'It's cool—we look beyond ourselves and get right to God's work.' We attract those who want an interactive and serving experience focused on God's grace and glory."

"Well, brother," Tim continued, "that represents some genuine heartfelt serving. Lil, where's your heart on all this?"

"My heart's really in the small-group ministry," asserted Lil. "The Gathering has Serve Groups, Pods, and Life Groups—all serving a different purpose and different age groups, but they all lead to missional. Stewardship has continued to increase proportionately with the focus on spiritual growth. A greater faith involvement has generated more time, talent, and treasure to do God's work. And I think we should add 'testimony' to that list."

"What a great addition to our worship services in the Village!" T exclaimed. Then he complimented 2J: "JJ, you're the man! You were responsible for integrating testimony or witnessing to our worship setting every weekend."

"It's just a natural," JJ insisted, "People like me want to tell their faith story, but we usually don't get invited or we chicken out because no one else is doing it. You know—giving our testimony at SEG is now a normal thing. Man, it's still hard to get up there, but it feels so good. It's radical! Man, it's the same feeling that I had on the streets when I knew King was watching my back.

"Hey, the Boss Man shook me loose for coffee a couple weeks ago—that means I paid. He's done a lot for me, and he's a real hero. He told me about losing his wife to some crazy cancer. Dude, he said when you came along and asked him to be part of the Disciples Group, he remembered almost rejecting your offer—his grief was taking him down. Boss also said he had no confidence without his talented wife—not having children also took him to a very lonely place." T started to say something when JJ interrupted.

"There's more, man! His exact words were, 'Without Pastor T and God, I would have faded into the woodwork.' We talked about our great relationship also."

"Wow," Tim intervened, "it's nice to share those intimate feelings and appreciation for each other. Some people never experience that!"

Lil added, "*As We Go Ministries* would never have happened without Van. But JJ, you are a central influence—God sent you to bring us all together. It also took resources from an entire community to create the network of serving ministries now in place."

"Nah! I just went on the ride. Hey, how did you get so many people like me that didn't like church to come to Second-Effort Gathering?"

Pastor enumerated, "Enthusiasm, creativity, relevance, interaction, theme, openly witnessing, need for each other, and an outward serving focus. The younger crowd likes the topical theme for the service and the messages presented in a four to six-week series. I can see why they like the format. I like it, too. Their life journey with God is more than a Bible story."

Gwen asked, "JJ, why did you finally consent to attending a worship service?"

JJ confessed, "My heart is in God's Word now, but you probably would have never gotten me in any church without great music and creative effects. It's awesome! I've watched Kyle and Dex coordinate the visual effects combining video, slides, live skits, puppetry, and this thing they call Square 'D'—the video clip production with four guys approaching a worldly issue from four perspectives, contrasting a worldly view with a Godly view."

"Yeah, Kyle's the mind behind this unique ministry," cited Pastor T. "He still keeps in touch with Phil, but his real mentor is Todd. They are almost like blood brothers. Todd's given a lot of support to Kyle's family also."

"T, what kinds of involvement are you experiencing in the Village worship?" asked Tim.

"Second-Effort Gathering can claim an average of 420 in attendance every weekend, with 70 percent of those staying for the small-group discussions. This doesn't count the hundreds of young people on campus who are in the social small-group ministry called 'Pods.' It all began when Phil started meeting a couple times a week in the Village, sitting around a table with a cup of coffee or a beverage and some snacks and sharing thoughts on a Christ-centered life. For many, this is what brought them into the church—and the music is compelling, too. Right, JJ?"

"Leah does a great job helping me to coordinate the music praise portion. People are genuinely happy as they sing praise. You know, dude—they smile! I like our band name—'Praise Gang.' Uh, right now we have about twenty in the gang."

"JJ's been so successful with his music and the business," T continued. "Van helped him set up the *As We Go* Foundation. All proceeds from his album sales go into the foundation and are used for missional projects all over the world. JJ, you have to be proud."

"Yeah—that's been a blast. The first money went to One Punch and his inner-city ministry. Another source of revenue to the foundation is the Square 'D' sales of their video skits. Kyle heads up the online sales effort."

"What is hugely different in the *As We Go* concept verses our traditional church culture?" asked Tim.

"Please let me," insisted JJ with enthusiasm. "Sometimes I roll things off my back with humor to avoid injury to my ego, but I would like to take a stand on this one. I have to say that discipling others comes down to one thing: relationships. We have all these things going on to help people, but the main thing in helping people is getting them to trust you enough to talk about their hurt. Pastor Dude showed me his love and introduced me to God's love. After I understood what was happening, I tried to relate to others in the same way, and guess what? It wasn't hard. The words 'as we go' came to life when I knew I could share Jesus every hour of every day with how I treated others. As I went to my music supplier, I created relationships, my music gigs gave me opportunity, and when I visited One Punch's gym, I developed more Christian relationships. That's the thing that has caught fire in the Village ministry. Everyone is doing it wherever they go."

Lil clapped and said, "Go, JJ! You make us proud."

JJ placed his hand on T's shoulder, saying, "I had better get back to the celebration. Our Praise Gang is up pretty soon. Thanks for the pizza, you guys. Love ya!" JJ gave everyone a hug, and then he headed back to the party.

"See you tomorrow, JJ." Pastor turned to Tim and asked, "How is God messing with your life?" The four talked for another twenty minutes about personal challenges. Tim shared, "My entire ministry is all about relationships as I deal with disabled veterans. Actually, my disability has helped to tear down the barriers JJ was talking about. My brother, you have partnered with God to open the hearts of so many by building up imperfect people to be disciples. I am not only impressed: I am proud—and Dad would be proud." They embraced each other and promised to keep in touch.

"It's time we hit the road," asserted Gwen. "This has been an awesome day. God is good."

The foursome headed toward the van as they expressed their feelings for each other. Pastor T requested they huddle for prayer. It was hard for T to say good-bye, but he was grateful for his brother's involvement in his life. As the couple pulled out, Tim rolled down his window and yelled, "Hey brother, your turn—come and visit us."

Pastor T and Lil wandered back to the Village, where a crowd had gathered to participate with the Praise Gang.

T started thinking about the next day's meeting with some VIPs from other colleges. They were scheduled to discuss using the Village project as a model for providing ministry in their communities.

Pastor leaned over to Lil, saying, "God has only started to use us! To think I spent all those years preaching salvation every weekend and just assumed the congregation would understand Christian obedience and responsibility. JJ and the other young people have given us valuable insight as to how to make disciples."

LOOKING FOR MEANING:

1. What reasons can you think of for Pastor T saying that counting those who are growing spiritually is a better form of measurement than counting those attending church?

2. Pastor said that he learned a lot about empowerment because it was not just turning people loose to do what they wanted to do. What did he mean?

3. Can you find some examples of interactive ministry in the conversation?

Chapter 17—Scope of Influence!

"Companions as we are in this work with you, we beg you, please don't squander one bit of this marvelous life God has given us. God reminds us, I heard your call in the nick of time; the day you needed me, I was there to help."

2 Corinthians 6:1 *(Message)*

God's followers radiate the influence of the Holy Spirit. As we go, working together in this life, we expand His scope of influence on others.

Chapter 17 relates the influence of one person who was inspired by the Holy Spirit to be the mind, hands, and voice of Jesus.

Scope of Influence!

Lil and T were having breakfast in their sun room, and T was mentally planning the day's meeting about using the Village project as a model in other locations. Those who would be attending were very influential representing church, community, and education. He was carrying his dishes to the sink when his phone rang. Pastor didn't recognize the number on his cell display.

"Good morning, this is Pastor T."

The calm, deliberate voice on the other end proceeded to explain a situation to Pastor. Lil noticed the worried expression on T's face and how intense his body language had become. So far, Pastor hadn't said a word, but he sat down at their dining room table, still listening. His fingers were repeatedly going through his hair. At this point, Lil knew there was something wrong. She sat alongside him and put her hand on his shoulder. Finally, with urgency in his voice, Pastor said, "Thank you for the personal call. I'll be right there." Pastor hung up the phone and put his head down, then looked at Lil with tears welling in his eyes.

Lil asked, "What happened?"

"It's JJ," he responded emotionally. "They found him lying on the sidewalk outside the Village building. I have to go to the hospital!"

"I'm going too! I'll drive," asserted Lil, "and you can explain on the way what happened."

They hopped in the Silver Streak and raced to the nearby hospital. T explained, "There was a lot of blood from an apparent bullet wound to the head. They thought he was dead, but the paramedics arrived, used a portable defibrillator, and revived him. They said he has a very weak heartbeat. One witness said that three guys opened fire on JJ from across the street and then ran through the park when JJ went down. The EMT unit was just about to leave the scene on its way to the hospital with JJ. I think we can get to the hospital before they do."

Pastor T called Van. In complete shock, Van said that he and Liz were having breakfast near the hospital and would come immediately. Lil dropped T off at the emergency entrance and parked in the adjacent lot. Pastor rushed to the emergency overhead door, where they had just started to transfer JJ's limp body onto a cart. Medical personnel were waiting to rush him into the OR. T grabbed JJ's lifeless hand and ran alongside the cart down the hall.

Liz and Van had also arrived and were running to catch up. The medical staff motioned the threesome to stay in the emergency waiting room while they hurried down the hall toward surgery. Pastor made the sign of the cross on JJ's forehead while Liz kissed JJ on the cheek with tears pouring from her eyes. By that time Lil had caught up. They all stepped aside as they watched JJ wheeled through the double doors into surgery.

They huddled with their arms firmly hugging the person next to them. Pastor prayed with a sense of urgency in his voice. Each of them followed with their own petition for JJ's life. Liz completely broke down, crying uncontrollable tears. Lil led her into the family waiting room. Everyone sat in complete silence, except for occasional sobbing, staring at the floor and offering more prayers to their loving God. Lil called Ags with the sad news.

About forty-five minutes later, Joe, Dee, and Ags rushed into the waiting room. Ags was on her phone trying to reach Oz who was driving a load cross-country. Ags left a message to call her back but didn't say what it was about. Not one person asked what happened. The concern was focused on JJ's survival.

The double doors opened, and a person in blue surgical scrubs walked toward them. It was Tom. He said Vi was on her way and he would be part of the team doing the surgery.

"We called in a brain surgeon who is prepping right now. I want to give you a heads up. JJ is in tough shape. It looks like he got hit with three bullets and has lost a lot of blood. He's only hanging on by a thread—it doesn't look good." Looking at everyone, Tom said, "Please say your prayers for JJ and for the surgical team."

Tom turned and went back into surgery. There was more sobbing and some deep sighs as those gathered tried to get emotions under control. There wasn't much talking—most everyone sat with hands folded and looking down. Vi entered without saying a word; she hugged everyone and joined the group in silent meditation. It seemed like hours, but no one broke the silence. There was just prayer and deep thought and concern for JJ.

Lil's thoughts went to the evening at their house when she gave JJ his first Bible. She could still see his smile of appreciation and his eyes watering as he accepted the book. She somehow knew that God, the Holy Spirit had already started working in JJ's heart. It was comforting to Lil to know that JJ had developed such a strong relationship with God.

Ags was thinking about the after-church breakfast with Lil and Pastor and how that relationship led to knowing JJ. She recalled the look on JJ's face when he saw One Punch the night of the gathering at Pastor's house. It was an expression of so much respect and love for this man who had a big influence on JJ's life. She had a dream that same night that JJ took her by the hand into this boxing gym, and the two of them got down on their knees with all these young people. JJ had their attention and said to them that Ags was his friend and that she was also a friend of Jesus. In her dream, he asked the young people, "Do you want Jesus to be your friend?" All of the kids responded by rushing over to Ags and hugging her. She woke up crying, and she had felt a close attachment to JJ and others like him ever since.

Vi recalled feeling so embarrassed by her selfishness as she heard JJ tell his story about life on the streets. It was probably the point when she felt she had to use her talents to help and love others. She remembered there was compelling attraction, almost like something was leading her to think about the needs of others and not her own.

Ags' phone broke the silence in the room. Ags picked up, but before she could answer, Oz asked, "Ags, did something happen to JJ?"

"Yes, Oz, but I didn't mention JJ when I called. How did you know?"

"Oh, God, this can't happen!" Oz's voice was trembling as he said, "I just pulled my rig off the road, and my whole body is shaking." Taking a deep breath, Oz continued, "before you tell me what's going on, I have to tell you what just happened. You might think I'm cracking up."

Urgently motioning the others in the room to listen, Ags switched the phone to external speaker. She shrugged her shoulders like she didn't know what Oz was going to say. "Try to calm down, Oz, and explain what happened."

Oz started to relate a strange experience from an hour before, about the same time JJ was shot. "I was rolling down the interstate, and it started raining for no reason—just enough to use the wipers and pay extra attention to the road. JJ's face appeared out of nowhere. It looked like he was sitting on the hood of my truck. I blinked, and he was still there smiling at me. I wiped my eyes to clear them, and he was giving me a 'thumbs-up.' I stopped the wipers and I thought I heard his voice telling me, 'I saw the King. Not my street buddy, but the real King—God! He is for real!' I turned the wipers back on, and the image was gone and it had stopped raining.

"I just thought I was dreaming with my eyes open, but I saw it—it was JJ. I got really spooked and pulled off the road. I'm sitting here shaking, with JJ's image and his words burned in my head—I am a complete basket case. I just knew something had happened. Is it JJ? How bad is it? Please God..."

Ags held the phone to her mouth and told Oz the details. Oz asked Ags to put him back on speaker phone so he could talk to the group.

"I wish I were there to be with all of you." Oz was obviously shaken. His voice filled with grief, he said, "Words can't express my feelings right now. JJ's image in my head is that of celebration about seeing God." Almost breaking down, he gasped, "I just love that kid. I'll join you in prayer. Love you all!"

Before Oz hung up, a nurse came into the room and said she had an update from surgery. At that point the surgery was going well, but JJ was just barely hanging on. They had revived his heart twice already. Dr. Tom said to keep praying!

Her phone still turned on, Ags asked, "Oz, did you hear that? Please take care of yourself."

"Yes! Yes!" responded Oz. "I won't budge until I hear from you—I'll keep praying!"

The room returned to its silence, with frequent sobs and deep breaths. Van was holding Liz's hand as he recalled when JJ first called him "Boss Man." That was JJ telling him he was an okay guy. Van always felt good when JJ called him Boss. It meant that they had a solid relationship. Van vividly remembered the opening day of JJ's business. JJ wasn't nervous about how many people would come in or how much money would be in the till. He was, however, a basket case wondering if he would be able to relay the feeling that he wanted to help his customers. Van always related JJ's helping and serving attitude to how the church should be. JJ somehow knew how to emulate the attitude of Jesus.

Liz, wiping her eyes and putting her head on Van's shoulder, couldn't help but think about Joey and JJ's talks. On his knees, JJ would say, "Tell me a story, Joey." Joey would respond by telling him a Bible story she had read. JJ would quiz her until Joey would start giggling. She would hug JJ and say that he was too old for her stories.

JJ taught Joey guitar, but he was more family than a teacher. Liz often thought that maybe she was the mother who JJ never had. He confided some of his real fears that he normally covered up by joking. She remembered him telling her how homesick he felt on the streets. He couldn't figure that out because he really never had a home life. She was so touched when he said that feeling disappeared because he had her to talk to and because he felt close to Jesus.

By then about three hours had passed since they wheeled JJ into the OR. Pastor was up and walking around, placing his hand on everyone's shoulders and trying to be of some comfort. Todd and Leah came in and said they had just heard. Pastor gave them an update that it was serious and a matter of JJ fighting for his life. Todd and Leah hugged everyone and settled in their chairs, where they fought tears and prayed for JJ.

Leah mostly remembered when JJ first belted out his song, "God Sent Me Angels." She couldn't help recalling the feeling she had that night. His voice was so convincing, and she had goose bumps on her arms. His song also made her feel like God's angels were wrapping their arms around her. She felt so safe and loved while JJ was singing and she was hanging on every word. JJ had become a dear friend when they started the church. She thought, "He was sent by God for those special moments in my life."

Leah nudged Todd, who had his head down, asking, "Are you okay?" He responded very quietly, "Not really! What makes a person shoot another person? I don't get it!" He put his head back as his memory went to the launching of the Village project. He remembered that he was a little jealous of JJ because the guy was so talented and Leah was completely taken by his music. Then he really got to know JJ in the weeks that followed.

Under his breath, Todd said, "This street guy was the genuine Christian." Todd wondered how JJ could turn out like that when other people who have all the advantages turn out so lukewarm in their faith. Still slumped over, he suddenly realized the impact JJ had on his life. He brought out the best in everyone. Not once in that five-year period did JJ ever think about himself. It was all about helping people around him. Todd's thought was, "God, You have led me into the ministry, and I never realized that You also sent JJ to be a friend, inspire the creativity in me, and come alongside of me when I needed encouragement." A few big tears dropped to the floor. Leah tried to comfort him by rubbing the back of his neck.

Todd's thoughts were interrupted by his cell phone. He quietly answered. The party must have asked about JJ. Todd's reply was, "His condition is really bad. We are at the hospital and JJ is still in surgery. Will the two of you pray really hard? I'll catch up to you later."

Todd told the group that it was Kyle and Dex. They had just heard and were between classes at the college.

Joe and Dee were very quiet. Dee leaned over and whispered into Joe's ear, "Remember what JJ said to us after the small-group meeting?" Joe's lip quivered as though he were holding back the tears. He put his head in his hands and relived that moment with JJ.

When everyone was refilling their refreshments at Oz and Ags' house, JJ had approached Joe and said, "Hey, man, hang in there—second chances is what God is all about. Sometimes our mouth reacts faster than our brain. I've been there too many times myself. What really counts is that the two of you have a giant heart—you make a good team. God will use you to do great things. I love you guys!" Joe remembered how reassured he felt because this street hero had made an effort to talk to him.

Pastor T had already cancelled all of his appointments for the day. Some of his disciples and a staff member from church would cover for him at the VIP meeting.

T looked around the room. He couldn't help but think to himself how awful everyone looked—swollen and red eyes, devastated expressions frozen on faces, and total sadness. Pastors are supposed to have the right words at a time like this, he thought. But I feel the same way they do, and I probably look as bad, too.

He cleared his throat and said, "If you're like me, the past three hours you've done some serious thinking about JJ and his relationship with you. You may have even found things in yourself that you are not too proud about. JJ probably noticed those things in each of us, but he maintained a sense of humor and remained humble even when he had real reason to boast, and eventually we all felt better about ourselves because he lived his life to be there for each of us.

"I chose to talk about JJ just now in past tense—like he's never coming back. That does not mean I'm giving up hope. I keep thinking about Oz sitting on the side of the road and seeing an image of JJ at the very same time that JJ was shot. Could that be coincidence? Oz had no reason to be thinking about JJ at that moment. What were the smile and the 'thumbs-up' about? Why did Oz hear JJ say that he saw the King, his Lord and Savior?

"My take on this is that God is in control right now. God's hearing our prayers, and He knows the kind of impact JJ had on each of us and on everything that has been accomplished with *As We Go Ministries*. God gave JJ to us with a plan. God made certain we all got connected to JJ in different capacities. God used all our gifts to rally around JJ to accomplish that plan and to serve God in ways we never thought were possible. We know God hasn't taken him from us yet. Let's have faith in knowing God will do what is best. Although we don't know if God's plan for JJ is complete, we can be assured that God is pleased that JJ helped us to love Him and each other. If JJ does leave us, he would want us to remember him the way the image came to Oz, happy and praising God. He would also say, 'Hey, dudes, don't worry about me. God has work for you.'"

A voice from the waiting room door said, "Amen, brother!" T turned to see One Punch. They embraced each other affectionately. Lil thought to herself, smiling, it's wonderful to see a priest and a minister having so much respect for each other.

One Punch hugged everyone in the room. He threw his broad shoulders back and his voice boomed as he announced that the three kids who shot JJ were in police custody. They were from a gang that was upset that JJ was mentoring two of their former members. The two who were being mentored were also meant to be a target.

"Let me say that JJ and I had a lot of talks over the last five years. When we got together we pretty much said anything that came into our minds. He told me stories about each of you and how he'd never be able to pay you back for all the love and help you gave him. He never saw himself as having much of an influence on you, until one day he asked me, 'Is it possible that God somehow used me to connect all these people? It seems like they all have done so much for me, but in that process they have become connected to each other.' He didn't see it as him having an influence but as God using him to connect you together to build His kingdom.

"In our last discussion, he said he was on a mission to get Liz and Van married. In his words, 'Liz and Van are like God just lowered them from heaven to be a couple! They are like two people I've never had in my life. I hope they know how much I love them. And when Joey calls me Uncle JJ, my heart skips a dozen beats.'"

One Punch turned to Pastor T and said, "Bro, you can do no wrong in JJ's eyes. You have to know that you are my hero also for taking care of one of my kids." One Punch moved on to each person and told them individually how JJ loved them.

Everyone got quiet as they heard a door open and footsteps in the hallway. Tom appeared in the doorway, removing his surgical cap and lowering his mask. Vi ran to him and hung onto his arm. He wasn't smiling, and it looked like he didn't know what to say.

Words finally came out as Tom confirmed, "Surgery was successful, but it will take a miracle for JJ to pull through. The one bullet we removed in his brain did a lot of damage. The other two are not life threatening, but he's lost a lot of blood. Right now he is getting some help breathing and we are monitoring his heart closely. In surgery his heart stopped twice, so we are concerned because of the trauma he experienced. He received six units of blood. And for now we are keeping him in a controlled coma until the swelling subsides in his brain."

Tearing up a bit, Tom continued. "As a doctor I have to remove my emotions and not allow anything to affect my performance in surgery. This was tough! Knowing JJ as a Christian and friend brought many thoughts into my head. I intentionally dismissed them until I started to walk down to you folks. We should consider ourselves fortunate to be associated with a person like JJ. Also, God gave us each other. I want you to know that I'm grateful that JJ brought us together. At this time it's important we lean on one another for support and praise God for His love. If I know JJ, he would want us to celebrate God's love.

"It will be a good sign if JJ makes it through the night. Even then he won't be out of the woods."

Just then someone motioned Tom back into the hallway. He rushed out of sight and was gone for about five minutes.

When Tom reappeared, his face had lost its color. Everyone's eyes were fixed on him as he walked back into the room. He put his arm around Vi and reached out with both hands as though to ask that everyone stand and join hands. Everyone complied, waiting for Tom to say something.

Tom slowly shook his head from side to side and said, "JJ died at 11:05, just four minutes ago. God's plan for JJ is complete!"

Everyone's reaction was the same: first, the silence of the shocking news, then a muscle reaction resulting in a tighter grip on the person next to them, and finally a burst of tears. Liz went to her knees still clinging to Van and Leah. Everyone followed.

Kneeling, Pastor T increased his grip with Lil and Ags, trying to find strength.

"God, we don't have Your understanding." Engaging a conversation with God, Pastor T prayed. "We are Your people kneeling in Your presence asking, 'Why?' Why did JJ have to leave us so soon? We know JJ's tragic death is part of Your plan. It hurts, even though we are thankful that JJ is with You, the King, his Lord and Savior. JJ is standing before You, giving a 'thumbs-up' with You saying, 'Well done, good and faithful servant.' We receive comfort in those words.

"Your presence in this room right now is evidenced by the love we all feel for You and our friend, JJ. These hands so tightly secured join us together in this moment of grief. You made our loyalties and friendships possible through JJ, that street kid who came into our lives from nowhere and captured our hearts. Lord, we thank You for the privilege of knowing and working with JJ to glorify You and Your name.

"You used JJ to unify us for Your command of making disciples. We must realize that our work is not done, or everything You have done through JJ would be in vain. God, we lean on You for that strength, courage, and wisdom to continue the ministry so it honors You and JJ.

"JJ, we know that you are able to see us right now. As you might put it, 'Dudes, you're kind of a mess! Don't you know you have work to do?' We realize that there's plenty of unfinished work to be done, but right now we've lost someone very dear to us. There's a time for us to grieve and then a time to finish the work you started.

"We ask You, God, to lead us so that we use our gifts effectively to maintain and build up Your kingdom. JJ, peace be with you, dude!

"In Jesus' name we pray—Amen."

LOOKING FOR MEANING:

1. Each person had their thought about JJ. What was your thought?

2. In retrospect, what do you see as God's plan that JJ was to fulfill?

3. What is the significant message in this story? Are you doing something about it?

Notes

[1] David Murrow, *Why Men Hate Going to Church* (Nashville, TN: Thomas Nelson, Inc., 1982).

[2] Rev. Barry J. Keurulainen.50 Days Ablaze! (Cabot, PA: Rev. Barry J. Keurulainen, 2005).

[3] *Passion of the Christ*, directed by Mel Gibson, with performances by James Caviezel and Maia Morgenstern (20th Century Fox, 2004).

[4] Thom S. Rainer and Eric Geiger, *Simple Church* (Nashville, TN: B & H Publishing Group, 2006).

[5] See www.goodreads.com/author/**quotes**/1538.**Stephen R Covey.**

[6] Charles Dickens, *Oliver Twist* (England: Richard Bentley, 1838).

[7] Charles Dickens, *The Christmas Carol* (England: Chapman and Hall, 1843).

www.ingramcontent.com/pod-product-compliance
Lightning Source LLC
LaVergne TN
LVHW051546070426
835507LV00021B/2433